TURMOIL IN THE TEMPLE

You cannot counsel DEMONS out, or medicate them out, Jesus said, **"CAST THEM OUT!"**

Don Dickerman

The scriptural principles are clear and simple and are outlined in this fascinating book . . . a follow up to **SERPENTS IN THE SANCTUARY**

Turmoil in the Temple, by Don Dickerman
ISBN # 0-89228-172-3

Copyright ©, 2002
by Don Dickerman

Published by
Impact Christian Books, Inc.
332 Leffingwell Ave.,
Kirkwood, MO 63122
314-822-3309

TURMOIL IN THE TEMPLE

FOREWORD:

When I was a Pastor of a church in the Dallas-Fort Worth area, (First Baptist of Colleyville), it was my privilege to witness Don Dickerman at work with one of our people who had requested prayer for healing and deliverance. As he says in his book, it was something quite unlike that which movies or media would have you believe.

In attendance were the recipient of prayer for deliverance, that person's parents and a small number from our congregation who were praying silently as Don spoke to the individual. Don was quietly spoken and outlined to the person what he was going to do and then proceeded. At the conclusion he closed the session with prayer. I visited the family the following day to ensure that all was well, only to be met by the father who claimed that his wife (the mother of the one prayed for) was a totally transformed person!!For years the mother had suffered from a negative, depressed attitude and during the prayer for her adult child, standing in the background, she had experienced a dramatic deliverence and life transformation.

The Apostle John tells us that "the reason the Son of God appeared was to destroy the devil's work" 1 John 3:8.

Professor John P. Newport writes. . . "It is the contention of C.K. Barrett, James Kallas, George Ladd and other evangelical scholars that the demonology-eschatology motif is dominant - constituting some three fourths of the material in the first three Gospels and Paul. This means that the New Testament teaches that satanic forces have a measure of real control in the world.

The former Anglican Bishop of Exeter has pointed out that in Western countries today, the widespread apostasy from the Christian faith, accompanied by an increasing recourse to black magic and occult practices, is revealing the presence and the power of evil forces and the contaminating influence of an evil atmosphere in particular places and environments. The need, therefore, for the restoration of the practice of exorcism to its proper place is becoming steadily more urgent and more evident.

It is encouraging to note that a number of prominent theologians are emphasizing the biblical perspective on demonology. These include Karl Heim, Gustaf Aulen, Gustaf Wingren, G.C. Berkouwer, Helmut Thielicke, and Eduard Thurneysen. Some psychiatrists and medical men, including A. Lechler, Thomas V. Moore, Bernard Martin, as well as psychologists like Charles Corcoran, also affirm the existence of supernatural demonic powers. A prominent theologian, Thurneysen, states that the demonic view of illness and sin in the Bible is not to be regarded as surpassed by modern psychology and psychotherapy. Whatever psychopathic phenomena may come to light through psychological probing, they are not the primary cause of man's trouble according to biblical thought. Rather, they are the reflection and refraction of that metaphysical bondage to the powers of darkness.

Oftentimes there is a confusion between demon influence, demon subjection and demon possession. The marks of demon possession are very extreme and quite rare. Demon subjection is perhaps more common. The marks of demon subjection are much less extreme than demon possession. Alfred Lechler suggests some of the characteristics of demon subjection: nonreceptivity to divine things, religious doubt, inaptness of true knowledge of sin, inability to concentrate in Bible reading and prayer, persistent lack of peace, inner unrest, temper bursts, blasphemy, depression, and suicidal thoughts. With these marks is joined various compulsions toward drunkenness, sexual immorality, falsehood, theft, smoking, and drugs."

What Don is writing about in this book is Biblical and expresses the ministry of Jesus, His commission to the twelve, then the seventy and what was normal activity in the Book of Acts.

Michael Green in his book "Evangelism in the Early Church" cites Eusebius, Ambrose, Cyprian and others who saw that the ministry of deliverence was an important aid to evangelism in the first three centuries of the early church. These named church fathers also had Baptismal prayers of demon renunciation as the norm for Baptismal services.So this is a book about a ministry, exercised by our Lord, the Apostles and the early Church. Don continues quietly and humbly to evidence the power of the Gospel in the Person of our Precious Savior and Lord "to set the captives free."

May I suggest you buy three copies. One for yourself and 2 for pastors, who as they read will know immediately of people in their congregation who also need to experience "the Freedom with which Christ has set us free."

Brian Willersdorf
International Evangelist
Sidney, Australia

Brian has been called the
"Billy Graham of Australia"

INTRODUCTION

I hope you have read SERPENTS IN THE SANCTUARY, it will certainly make this book have more meaning for you. There is so much more to be written about the subject of spiritual warfare and the reality of the demonic kingdom of Satan. I believe the Church is about to enter into a new wave of spiritual activity. Deliverance ministers are being raised up now to wage warfare and bring freedom to God's children. The Lord Jesus is coming for a Bride that is without spot, wrinkle or blemish, and that is not the condition of the Church today. God's people are sick. The hospitals have as many Christians occupying their beds as non-Christians. This ought not to be. Divorce is as rampant in the Church as outside of it. This is an ugly blemish.

God's people are being "beaten up" by the enemy and it is because of ignorance! No believer need fear the enemy. No child of God should be retreating from the forces of hell. None of the Body of Christ need experience demonic oppression, but we do!

We MUST learn who we are in Christ. We must learn our authority and privileges in the Name of Jesus Christ. Pastor's have a mandate on their lives to teach the people.

Jesus admonished Peter to "Feed His sheep." The sheep are hungry for the Word, the sheep need protection and are vulnerable to the enemy, because shepherds are neglecting the sheep. The sheep must know how to protect themselves. Following the shepherd is not always enough, the shepherd must do some fighting!

I am constantly amazed at the reluctance of pastors to equip the people to do battle. Whatever excuse one may give, it is inexcusable to leave the people in ignorance. The demons have done a good job of intimidating the pastors. The book is somewhat of a manual to help pastors and Christian leaders to come to the front, to "step up" and prepare the people for warfare. I believe there will be great accountability to those who neglect this important part of God's message.

TURMOIL

IN THE

TEMPLE

Chapter 1

TURMOIL IN THE TEMPLE

"And (Jesus), said unto them, It is written My house shall be called the house of prayer but you have made it a den of thieves." Matthew 21:12

What first comes to your mind when you think of there being "turmoil in the temple"? Do you think of the many conflicts that arise within organized religion? Do church-splits come to your mind? What about the restless congregation that is never satisfied with its pastor?

All of these things should not be but we all know that it is far too common.

However, that is not my subject. What I do want to discuss might well eliminate some of those problems within the organized local congregations. I am talking about *your* temple and my temple. *"Our earthly house"* as Paul calls it in 2 Corinthians 5. He also refers to us as a tabernacle. *"For we that are in this tabernacle do groan, being burdened;..."*

In 1 Corinthians 3:17 the word declares, *"Know you not that you are the temple of God, and that the Spirit of God dwells in you."* Clearly the scripture indicates that we, as believers, are indwelt by the Spirit of God. Where does He live? I mean, does He occupy our entire being? Where does the Holy Spirit abide in us? We are a trinity, a spirit that has a soul that lives in a body.

11

Does the Holy Spirit live in our flesh, our body? Does He live in our soul; that is, our mind, our will and emotions? Does He live in our spirit? Clearly He lives in our spirit. That is what is born again. Our spirit is eternal.

Liken the spirit of man unto the "Holy of Holies" in the Temple or Tabernacle. Only a high priest with a blood sacrifice could enter the "Holy of Holies. To enter with sin in his life would be certain death. He was entering into the very Presence of Jehovah God. Nothing unclean could be in God's Presence. The Holy Spirit of God lives in our *Holy of Holies*, our spirit.

The soul of man, which is our mind, will and emotions can entertain sin. Certainly uncleanness can and often does live in our soul. Obviously our flesh can indulge in sin. Uncleanness and unholiness must abide in the soul and flesh if it is in the human body. Our soul and our flesh would be the equivalent of the outer court and the holy place. The flesh must die daily, our mind, will and emotions must surrender to the Holy Spirit's direction and conviction in order to live a pleasing life unto the Lord. The Blood of Jesus must be applied to our sin, cleansing and covering it. The turmoil in the temple is the conflict that rages within us. The Holy Spirit cannot participate in our sin and evil deeds.

Paul describes this conflict in Romans chapter 7. He describes a war raging within him. The Holy Spirit showing him what is right, just and holy and the soul and flesh desiring that which is not. There is turmoil in the temple. Frank Hammond called it "Pigs in the Parlor."

Often people ask me how a demon could possibly be in a Christian if the Holy Spirit is there. My response is with a question, "How can sin and evil thinking be where the Holy Spirit is?" Sin is in the flesh, the mind, will and emotions. Turmoil is the result. Demons cannot enter the spirit of man, just as sin could not enter the Holy of Holies. But, demons can and do gain access to the flesh and soul of believers! This is a battle and it is not being discussed by most preachers. Hence, many Christians live defeated lives because they are not even aware of what the battle is.

Demonic oppression or demonization is common among believers. Obviously, it is not demon possession. Possession is ownership and we are owned by the Lord Jesus. We have been bought, purchased with a price. Possession is not the question! Demons gain access to the body or the soul by many different doorways. My experience is that they stay, until they are commanded to leave. They enter by deception and become "squatters" and they will take and take, until someone in the Name of Jesus Christ puts an end to it.

Jesus dealt with "Turmoil in the Temple." Remember when He went up to Jerusalem at the time of Passover and found the temple in turmoil? The time of celebration for the deliverance from Egypt. The commemoration of the shedding of innocent blood to bring protection for the people. The most holy of times for the Hebrews. And the temple was in disarray.

I want you to know that Jesus exercised His Authority! He called the temple *"my Father's house"* that makes it His house. He did not *invite* those who defiled the temple to leave. He did not *suggest* that it would be a good thing if they did. He demanded it! With force and heavenly authority He commanded the thieves to leave. He upset the place they had assumed in the temple. The Word of God says that *He drove them all out*! (John 2:13-17).

Luke's recording of this event quotes Jesus as saying, *"My house is the house of prayer; but you have made it a den of thieves."* (Luke 19:46). Luke also said that Jesus **cast** out them that bought and sold! "A den of thieves"? Indeed!

I have found many such dens of demons. They have all come to rob, steal, kill and destroy! Demons in believers are exactly that

13

. . . a den of thieves. They steal joy and peace, they rob relationships and health, spirit fruit is squelched. Demon spirits in believers must be dealt with just as Jesus dealt with those who caused turmoil in His temple. They must be driven out. They cannot be medicated out nor counseled out. He did not say to pray them out or read them out, neither did He suggest we sing or worship them out. He said to "cast them out"!

Jesus was offended that man would defile the very temple of God. It was the place for worship. Once the offenders were driven out the blind and the lame came and were healed of Him. I find that healing often takes place in the temple once it is cleansed. (Matthew 21:12-15).

Many are sick and are experiencing turmoil and defeat because of the unclean spirits that have invaded their temple. The conflict is real. The ugly, defeated demons are stealing from God's people. They have set up a kingdom of destruction in the very temple of God, the soul and flesh of believers. A nest of iniquity! A den of thieves! There is turmoil in the temple and Jesus came to drive out all that defiles His temple. Know you not that we are the temple of God!

Believers don't have to take it. I pray this book will be an eye-opener. I pray truth will be revealed so that you no longer have turmoil in the temple and that you can bring others to freedom in Christ Jesus.

Chapter 2

ARE WE DOING WHAT JESUS DID?

". . .God anointed Jesus of Nazareth with the Holy Ghost and power: who went about doing good, and healing all that were oppressed of the devil; for God was with Him."   Acts 10:38

I don't know the number of churches in the world, I'm sure the number is staggering. In each congregation there is an assigned preacher. In the pews of most churches there are several others ministers, who have expressed the call of God on their life. I wonder among this great number of servants how many have encountered evil spirits. Even more, I wonder how many resisted them in the mighty name of Jesus Christ?

I am well aware that pastors must preach a balanced message and that there are varying degrees of spiritual maturity in each congregation. I totally understand that deliverance is not "the" ministry, but it certainly <u>is part of</u> *"the"* ministry.

Some have referred to healing, deliverance and gifts of the spirit as "apostolic doctrine." Meaning that those gifts were for the apostles, not for the modern believer. I would simply say to that; then being born again was only for Nicodemus. The sermon on the mount was only for those present, etc. The argument is weak and only reflects the disbelief of the one making this claim.

I would guarantee every pastor that someone in your congregation needs deliverance. My guess is that most people in every congregation are in need of "oppression healing." The above Scripture is a wonderful description of what Jesus came to do. He came to bring relief from the oppressing powers of Satan. That, includes more than forgiveness of sin.

While pastors have for the most part ignored this message, it is nonetheless true. The Church today is weak, anemic, sick and in bondage. We are just like the unsaved, when it comes to sickness, divorce, and other areas of bondage. The reason, I believe, is simple, the message of freedom from demonic powers is not being preached.

Pastor, what will you do when your members start to come to you to ask for help in this area? If it has not already happened, it will. The numbers will increase, I assure you that you will not be able to escape it. Sure, you can send them to a counselor. You can recommend a Christian psychologist. But Jesus did not say "counsel them out" nor "medicate them out." Neither can you get them out by being more religious. You can't wish them out, nor will them out. Jesus said to "cast them out" and that is the role of the Church!

The battle is heating up. You cannot lead your Church where you have not been. You must bring your people out of spiritual bondage and teach them to walk in freedom and boldness. That's why I have written this book. I wish my pastor had taught me. I could have avoided so much pain. I could have helped my mother, who was tormented with demons. I could have helped my brother, who was in the grips of sickness and debilitating bondage from the enemy. I could have made a difference in so many lives. . . but no one told me. No one taught me. If Jesus came to "heal all that were oppressed of the devil," should we not let that same Jesus come alive in us? Should we not be advancing against the kingdom of darkness with all the authority Jesus has given us. Have we not been silent long enough?

A pastor said from the pulpit recently. "My son has been waking up every night in horror, he cries out in such fear. My wife and I would go to his room to try to calm him and talk him back to sleep. Sometimes he would walk in his sleep during these times of fright. I was downstairs studying one night when I heard his scream. As I walked to the stairs, it seemed the Holy Spirit said to me, *"How long are you going to take this? You know what it is. Deal with it."* The pastor said he climbed the stairs and picked up his screaming son. He cuddled him in his arms and addressed demons. "This is MY son. I command you in the Mighty Name of Jesus Christ, Leave him alone! Leave now and never return in Jesus Christ's Name."

He went on to say with a big smile on his face, "Ever since that night it has been nothing but zzzzzzzzzzz's, just peaceful sleep."

Why don't we teach the people what kind of authority we have in Christ? Pastor, I urge you first to get in the stream, get more than your feet wet. Jump in head first, plunge into the river! Experience firsthand Who Jesus is, and who you are in Christ. You can't teach it until you experience it. Spiritual warfare is more than knowing about Ephesians

6 and II Corinthians 10:4,5.

Power of attorney is legal, recognized authority one has received from another. Prior to my father's death he gave me power of attorney. Legal, court recognized, authority to act in his behalf. His authority became my authority. I could sign his name, make decisions in his name and it was honored! Jesus has given us POWER of attorney. *"Hitherto have you asked nothing in my Name, ask and you shall receive, that your joy may be full."* John 16:24

He sent out the seventy with power of attorney. He told the Church gathered after His resurrection, *"As my Father has sent me, even so send I you."* John 20:21. How did the Father send Him? With all power in both heaven and earth. All power was given unto Him by the Father. He gave it to us, as regards the spiritual world on this earth! Power to speak with authority to demon powers and to make them retreat. Power of life and death in our words. Authority over all the power of the enemy. I urge you to jump into this stream of anointing. It may cost you some thing, but it is worth it, whatever the cost!

God's people are sick. They are in spiritual bondage. I believe God is looking for deliverers. For men who will stand unashamed in the power and authority of the Lord Jesus and speak to set His People free!.

Chapter 3

WHO IS SATAN ANYWAY?

"Be sober, be vigilant; because your adversary the devil, as a roaring lion, walketh about, seeking whom he may devour: Whom resist stedfast in the faith, knowing that the same afflictions are accomplished in your brethren in the world."

Peter 5:8,9

Have you ever really given much thought to who Satan is? He is very likely not who you think he is. He has many names and titles given throughout Scripture. I'm not going to give you all of that here. I just want you to know he's a liar and a deceiver, and likely has you fooled about who he is. He has had some bad days in history and he has some bad days to come.

Knowing who we are in Christ is absolutely necessary if we are to be successful in spiritual warfare.

The above Scripture reveals quite a bit of information. We are to be on guard at all times. We are to remain alert and aware because. . .because the kingdom of darkness is looking for those that can be devoured! The demons are looking for whom they MAY devour. Since I am in Christ and have been given authority in the Name of Jesus Christ, I will not grant him permission; he is seeking whom he MAY devour. Who is he anyway, seeking to devour Gods children?

First, let's look at who he is not. Satan is not the opposite of God We have a real adversary, a very real enemy, in the devil! He is a liar and a loser and the power he has over believers is only in lies, threats and deceits. I am going to share a little of that message with you as an encouragement. If you ask the average man on the street who Satan is, you would likely hear that he is the opposite of God. He is evil, God is good and there is a conflict in the heavenlies that involves mankind. That one or the other influences us. This is a gross misconception. It is not even close to scriptural truth.

Satan is not the opposite of God, he is not even close. He is not omnipotent, omniscient, immutable nor omnipresent, GOD IS. God has no counterpart. Lucifer is the opposite of Michael, not God. God is in a league all by Himself. Satan is a created being, a fallen angel and is very limited in power. He was created as an archangel and was a magnificent creation called Lucifer. Possibly one of three archangels that included Gabriel and Michael. That he was an astounding creation is doubtless.

What is Satan's origin? It was God that was in the beginning, not Satan. God made everything. Satan created nothing. . .except rebellion! Is not the CREATOR always greater than the creation? Read the account of Lucifer in the following Scripture.

"Son of man, take up a lamentation upon the king of Tyrus, and say unto him, Thus saith the Lord GOD; Thou sealest up the sum, full of wisdom, and perfect in beauty. Thou hast been in Eden the garden of God; every precious stone was thy covering, the sardius, topaz, and the diamond, the beryl, the onyx, and the jasper, the sapphire, the emerald, and the carbuncle, and gold: the workmanship of thy tabrets and of thy pipes was prepared in thee in the day that thou wast created. Thou

art the anointed cherub that covereth; and I have set thee so: thou wast upon the holy mountain of God; thou hast walked up and down in the midst of the stones of fire. Thou wast perfect in thy ways from the day that thou wast created, till iniquity was found in thee. By the multitude of thy merchandise they have filled the midst of thee with violence, and thou hast sinned: therefore I will cast thee as profane out of the mountain of God: and I will destroy thee, O covering cherub, from the midst of the stones of fire. Thine heart was lifted up because of thy beauty, thou hast corrupted thy wisdom by reason of thy brightness: I will cast thee to the ground, I will lay thee before kings, that they may behold thee. Thou hast defiled thy sanctuaries by the multitude of thine iniquities, by the iniquity of thy traffick; therefore will I bring forth a fire from the midst of thee, it shall devour thee, and I will bring thee to ashes upon the earth in the sight of all them that behold thee. All they that know thee among the people shall be astonished at thee: thou shalt be a terror, and never shalt thou be any more" (Ezekiel 28:12)

Ezekiel speaks in this passage of the king of Tyrus. However, the passage has a double meaning. It describes the literal king of Tyrus, but also describes Satan. God, the creator made (literally "set") Satan to be full of wisdom and perfect in beauty. He was complete. God also "set" him in the garden of Eden. Remember, he was kicked out of heaven, he rebelled against God, he fought to be like God, to take over and he lost his first estate. He was kicked to this earth and was already present when man was created.

God covered him with every precious stone. Actually this list is the same as for the stones on the apparel of the high priest with the exception of three stones. The gold is spe-

21

cifically representative of kingly apparel. The Mercy Seat in the temple was made of pure gold. The idea of "workmanship" indicates that God made Satan for a specific service. Satan had tabrets (timbrels) and pipes (flute or horn, or organ) built into his body. The idea of "prepared" indicates these were designed by God with a specific purpose. Satan was to use these to lead the heavenly hosts in worship of God. God designed music for the purpose of worship. Satan was Heaven's worship leader. I suppose due to Satan's firing, that there's an opening in heaven for a worship leader. How would you like to have that job? We should practice for it while we are here. Worship Him from where you are.

Satan was the anointed cherub. The concept of "anointed" meant to be set apart for service unto God (see Exodus 30:26). The concept of "covered" may be compared to Isaiah 6:1-3 and Exodus 25:20. God said, "I have set thee so." Please notice who is in charge. God said that Satan was upon the holy mountain of God. This was the place set apart or exalted for God. Satan was in the presence of God walking up and down in the middle of the stones of fire. What an awesome sight this must have been!

I will cast thee as profane out of the mountain, says God. Satan was perfect in his ways, his thoughts and actions from the time God created him. Then iniquity was found in him. The word "iniquity" means perverseness or wickedness. Iniquity, we will learn is different from sin. We will see iniquity is also a "spirit" of evil. It is wickedness, the spirit that leads to sin. It is that same spirit which is passed to others through the permission of generational curse. Jehovah God bluntly says that Satan has sinned because iniquity was found in him. God is always in control!. *"I will* cast thee as profane out of the mountain of God." God said, "*I will destroy thee.*" Why? Satan began to look at his beauty and focus his attention on himself. Once, he had seen from God's perspective (true wisdom), but now that wisdom became darkened when he looked at himself.

Again, God declared his sovereignty. "*I will cast thee to the ground, I will lay thee before kings, that they may behold thee.*" Because of Satan's pride, God says that He will bring judgment upon Satan. Because of Satan's iniquity (perverseness - wickedness) and his spreading of that iniquity, God will judge him with fire. Satan's kingdom is made up of fallen angels. . .iniquity spirits! This is important to note in dealing with generational spirits (Exodus 20:5).

People who have given their lives to Satan, even some who have worshiped him and who once admired the beauty, power, and work of Satan will someday be astonished at him. People who also feared him, and Christians who refused to fight against him will see the horror of his shame and humiliation. They will see that he will never be as he once was. "*How art thou fallen from heaven, O Lucifer, son of the morning! How art thou cut down to the ground, which dids' weaken the nations! For thou hast said in thine heart, I will ascend into heaven I will exalt my throne above the stars of God: I will sit also upon the mount of the congregation, in the sides of the north: I will ascend above the heights of the clouds; I will be like the most High*" (Isaiah 14:12-14).

Lucifer is the original name given to the devil. The term "Lucifer" means the "shining one." This is interesting, because we can see that God created Lucifer (Satan) to reflect God's glory. However, now he only "appears" as an angel of light, but actually is the angel of darkness.

THE FIVE FOOLISH BOASTS OF SATAN

Satan in his pride and rebellion made some foolish boasts. Most preachers have spoken from this passage and called these boasts "The Five 'I Will's' of Satan."

1. *"I will ascend into heaven"* Perhaps the first seed of iniquity. He decides he will be like God and assumes to take the abode of God.

2. *"I will exalt my throne above the stars of God"* This is likely when he attempted to take control over all angels (Job 38:7).

3. *"I WILL cast thee to the ground . . ."* Ezekiel 28:17

4. *"I WILL lay thee before kings that they may see thee . . ."* Ezekiel 28:17

5. *"I WILL bring thee to ashes in the earth in the sight of all them that behold thee . . . and never shalt thou be any more."* Ezekiel 28:18, 19

God's simple response to this foolish boasting and rebellion is recorded in Isaiah 14:15-17

"Yet thou shall be brought down to hell, to the sides of the pit. They that see thee shall narrowly look upon thee, and consider thee, saying, Is this the man that made the earth to tremble, that did shake kingdoms; That make the world as a wilderness, and destroyed the cities

thereof; that opened not the house of his prisoners?"

When Satan's judgement is revealed people will marvel, not at his power, but the deceptiveness of appearing to have power. He was perfect . . . until iniquity was found in him! He was an awesome creation of God BUT, that's all he is, just a created being, he is one angel! Just one fallen angel! Since he is not omnipresent, he cannot be where I am and where you are at the same time. He is not a spirit that covers the earth. It is a grievous error to believe otherwise. God can, and is everywhere present at all times.

Do you think Satan has ever been to your house? I seriously doubt it. It is important that you read carefully what I am about to say. Since Satan can only be in one place at a time, I doubt that he has personally been to my home or to yours. While I am certain my name is known in the kingdom of darkness, I doubt that Satan knows my name. He cannot be but in one place at one time. My guess is that most of his time is spent in Washington, D.C. and influential capitals of the world. He is not omnipresent! But his demon powers roam about as a roaring lion, when Satan came before God concerning the life of Job, he confessed he had been *'going to and fro in the earth, . . . walking up and down in it.'* Job 1:7.

He is not omnipotent, all-powerful. As a matter of fact, he is very limited in his power and is always in subjection to Jehovah God. He had to ask God's permission to touch Job, because there was a hedge of protection that he could not penetrate. Not only did he have to seek permission, but God also set the limitations as to what he could and could not do. It is important to know he is not God's equal opposite! He's not even close.

Satan is <u>not</u> omniscient, all knowing. His knowledge is limited and he cannot know what God has not revealed to him. He can only know what is revealed in Scripture, or what Jehovah God allows him to know. Certainly demon powers know our tendencies and our past failures, but can only know our thoughts, if they have access to our mind by dwelling in our soul. I actually doubt that even then can they "read our minds." Do they know what you are going to do, or are about to do? Think back to the times you have started to pray or read your Bible and some distracting activity took place.

Satan is <u>not</u> immutable; rather he is the opposite. Always changing, lying and deceiving. What we must logically and spiritually deduce from this is that it is not Satan himself that we deal with, it is his demons. There is obviously a demonic hierarchy and we deal with some of the lowest ranking soldiers. You can imagine a line of reporting that goes through many demonic powers before it reaches Satan himself. Demons we deal with likely report to regional or territorial spirits. Spirits over communities, cities, counties, states, regions, countries, nations, hemispheres and the world system. Likely more complex than we can comprehend.

Without doubt, there is a system of rank and power in place. The powers that we deal with are on assignment from higher-ranking evil spirits. But let it suffice here to say, that Satan is not who most people think he is. He has had some bad days in his history and has some to come. Lets review a few of those bad days . . . we will consider 7 of those days.

He has had some bad days and he has some bad days to

come. He is a defeated foe, right now, this moment, he is defeated. It is important that we remember that Satan is a defeated enemy and only has power over us, that we give to him, that we yield. He was disarmed at Calvary, publicly humiliated. *"And having spoiled principalities and powers, he made a shew of them openly, triumphing over them in it."* Colossians 2:15

"He made a shew of them openly . . ." This is what the Romans would do, when they returned victorious from a battle. They would display the enemy in humiliation. They would glory in their victory by showing the enemy soundly defeated. Many times the victorious chariots would return with leaders of the opposing army strapped to the wheels as the chariots came into the city, they made a show of the defeated enemy. They gloried in their triumph. So did Jesus with the shed Blood and glorious resurrection! Jesus made Satan the 'Barney Fife' of the spirit world! He more or less said, 'you can keep your gun, but I'll take the bullets! He is a threat no more; fear, lies and deceit have become his power concerning believers. The power he has over believers is the lies we believe and Biblical ignorance we tolerate.

SEVEN BAD DAYS FOR THE DEVIL

Satan's first bad day is recorded in Isaiah 14:12-17. He was kicked from heaven to this earth. In all of Lucifer's magnificence, pride found a way into his life. It seems clear that he was the praise and worship leader in heaven. One third of the angels made up his heavenly choir. He deceived himself. He forgot he was the created, and not the Creator. He actually made a decision to be like God, has the clay power over the potter? Ridiculous is his self-deception.

The five "I will's" of Satan, as referred to earlier, indicate that Satan was given a will and made a very foolish choice. This makes me believe his own deception and pride blinded him. Regardless, it got him booted from heaven! Talk about a bad day! Kicked from heaven to this earth. This was more than a "bad hair day"; this was a baaad day! There is no real evidence, when in history this event took place. Likely, Satan's arrival on planet earth was the cause of the darkness. It is clear that he was already here, when man was created.

You see that while Satan is extremely deceptive and clever, he lacks real wisdom and understanding. In his foolish boasting he actually said that he would be like God. That is part of his lie today. Seeking the worship of men in luring them from worship of God. He still wants to rule! Someday when we see him for who he really is we will proclaim, *"Is this the man?"* (Isaiah 14:16,17). This is the one we feared, this is the one who caused all of the havoc? This is the destroyer? Notice also in the last phrase of verse 17 that he does not open the house of his prisoners!

If he, through his demonic kingdom, gets a person into bondage, there is no parole, there is no mercy, and he does not open the house of his prisoners. This is another reason Jesus came and took the keys from Satan. Jesus holds the keys of death and hell, but he also took the keys of the prison, (bondage to the kingdom of darkness), and gave them to the Church. Any believer, who stays in bondage, does so through ignorance or a choice to remain in the bondage.

But, back to his dismissal from the heavens. Talk about a demotion, he was reduced to the 'god of this world.' His domain was greatly diminished and he became the prince and power of the air, the ruler of darkness. He was greatly reduced in power, when God booted him from His Presence. When we look back and see him for who he really is, we will say, "*Is this the man . . . ?*" That was Satan's first bad day . . . it was a bad day for the devil when he got kicked out of heaven.

Look at this and rejoice. Jesus was present when Satan was booted to this earth, He told the seventy, which represent the Church, in Luke 10:18:

"I beheld Satan as lightening fall from heaven."

Do you realize what Jesus is saying? I know who he is, I know his power. I saw him fall, I was there when he was cut down to the ground, greatly reduced in power. I know all about him and his fall! Likely, it was Jesus who kicked Satan from heaven to this earth. Now understand the impact of His next words. Luke 10:19:

"Behold, I give unto you power to tread on serpents and scorpions, and over all the power of the enemy and nothing by any means shall hurt you."

Pretty awesome isn't it? I know who he is and I am giving YOU authority over him. This is absolutely an incredibly overlooked verse of Scripture. More on that later.

Satan's second bad day came, when he began to mess with God's creation. Apparently it really disturbed him that we, and not him, were created in God's own image. I like that it bothers him. He was already seeking whom he could devour. He was lurking about to destroy God's plan and purpose. He is called "the destroyer." You see, he was already on this earth, when man was created. He used his powers of deception and lied to Eve with the same lie he is spreading today. You will be like God . . . the seeds of new age and humanism were planted in the garden. The message is not new at all, and it's the oldest of all lies. Genesis 3:14,15

"And the Lord God said unto the serpent, Because thou hast done this, thou art cursed above all cattle, and above the beast of the field; upon thy belly shalt thou go, and dust shalt thou eat all the days of thy life: And I will put enmity between thee and the woman, and between thy seed and her seed; it shall bruise thy head, and thou shalt bruise his heel."

After man's fall, God showed up in the garden and cursed the serpent, He gave the promise of a Savior, who would crush his head . . . second bad day for the devil. Genesis 3:15 was a bad day for the devil!

The bad day was a promise for mankind that a Savior would someday crush Satan beneath His feet. A promise of a woman giving birth to the Son of God, God in the flesh. I'm sure Satan understood what was going to happen, but he did not know when. He didn't know how soon. . .and he didn't know how to prevent it. This bad day lasted four thousand years. Wondering and waiting. He likely did not know, until prophecies dating the Messiah's coming were revealed through the prophets.

He had four thousand years to anticipate this day. The day

he would bruise the Savior's heel, but would be crushed in the head, beneath His feet! He knew it was coming and couldn't stop it. Oh, that was a bad day, when he deceived man and received the promise of a Savior to be born that would crush his head, now that was a bad day.

I'm sure each time that one of God's prophets told of the Messiah's coming that Satan had nervous tremors. I believe he is having those now, knowing that his demise is getting closer with each passing day. For when Jesus returns for His Bride, Satan's day are literally numbered, he will have 1007 years before he is forever banished in the Lake of Fire. He gets a little more desperate with each day that brings us closer to the rapture!

The third bad day was not the birth of Jesus, but the baptism of Jesus. Many unusual events surrounded the birth of the Lord Jesus. An increase in heavenly activity with visitation from Holy Angels. A similar atmosphere that we will likely experience prior to His Second Coming. When Jesus was born, Satan used Herod to try to kill the long expected Messiah, but this was not possible. And I can tell you with great confidence that he cannot prevent what God may be birthing in your life! If you, or promises in your life, are anointed by the Hand of God, it will come to pass. Satan may hinder but never thwart the plans and purposes of God.

The birth of Jesus was not Satan's third bad day. Actually he has had many bad days down through heavenly history. The birth of Jesus was a continuation of the second bad day. It was intensifying. The third bad day, I believe, came when John baptized Jesus. This was the beginning of the end for Satan, and he knew it.

"And Jesus, when he was baptized, went up straitway out of the water: and, lo, the heavens opened unto him, and he saw the Spirit of God descending like a dove, and lighting upon Him:And lo a voice from heaven, saying, This is my beloved Son in whom I am well pleased. Then was Jesus led up of the Spirit into the wilderness to be tempted of the devil. And when He had fasted forty days and forty nights, he was afterwards an hungered. And the tempter came to Him . . ."   Matthew 3:16-4:3a

I can see this taking place. The Holy Spirit coming upon Jesus with power and directing Him to the wilderness for a face to face confrontation with Satan. It was like Satan was offering a challenge, 'Ok, let's you and me just get it on. I've been waiting 4,000 years for this day. I've got my best spiritual weapons ready for you. I imagine Jesus replying with something like this: 'Yeah, well first let me fast for 40 days and 40 nights, to make myself as weak as humanly possible, so this will be a little more even, because I'm about to beat you up one side and down the other! It won't even be close, it won't go into overtime, there will be no extra innings, I am going to beat you like the dog that you are!'

Jesus fought Satan on neutral ground in Matthew 4:1-10. Look at the result of that skirmish, that's all it was to Jesus, a skirmish. "Get thee hence, Satan" After Satan fired his best shots trying to defeat Jesus by causing Him to sin, Jesus spoke to him like the dog that he is . . . get out of here! He beat him up with the WORD of God and on the way to the main event at Calvary, he stomped on him time after time, healing the sick, casting out his demons, raising the dead, giving believers authority over all demon powers, including Satan himself, preaching the gospel to the poor . . . this was on the way to the main event. Third bad day for the devil! I see Satan leaving that confrontation with his ears laid back, his tail tucked between his legs and his rear dragging the ground, Jesus spoke to him like he was a dog. Get out of here!

Jesus defeated Satan with the Word. You, too, can know that when Satan fires his best shots at you and you stand on the WORD, victory is assured. When we resist, demons retreat. Not only that, after this skirmish, the Angels of God came and ministered to Jesus. They will come to you also. Keep standing on the WORD. The WORD defeats him, because the WORD is truth and demons are liars.

As Jesus continued toward the cross He was virtually beating on Satan and the kingdom of darkness daily. Three times he slapped death right in the face and spoke life to corpses! He raised the dead and, proclaimed that He would rise from the dead. All the way to the cross Jesus demonstrated that He alone is Lord. He conquered disease, demons and death and demonstrated His authority that would soon be given unto believers.

He revealed His authority over wind and waves, He walked on water and calmed seas, He spoke a curse to a tree and it died, He spoke to Lazarus and he lived. He said, *"Have faith in God. For verily I say unto you, That whosoever shall say to this mountain, Be thou removed, and cast into the sea; and shall not doubt in his heart, but shall believe that those things which he saith shall come to pass; he shall have whatsoever he saith."* Mark 11:22-23

What awesome words He spoke. Have faith in God. If you can believe, YOU can receive. Please note the "whosoever" in the above verse is the same "whosoever" that calls men to Christ. It includes any believer, not "special" believers. He poked at Satan all the way to the cross.

When the seventy returned from their appointed, anointed mission, (Luke 10:1-7), they marveled. Now you must know these were not the 12 disciples, nor were they their relatives, they certainly were not apostles, they obviously are representative of the Church today; they were "whosoevers" and He gave them authority. Look at the transaction in Luke 10:17-24.

"And the seventy returned again with joy, saying, Lord, even the devils are subject unto us through thy Name. (I tell you, when you experience the authority of Jesus' Name, you will have joy)

And He said unto them, I beheld Satan as lightning fall from heaven.

Behold, I give unto you power to tread on serpents and scorpions, and over all the power of the enemy; and nothing shall by any means hurt you. (Wow!)

Notwithstanding, in this rejoice not, that the spirits are subject unto you; but rather rejoice, because your names are written in heaven. (That I have given you authority over demons is a given, the big deal is that your name is written in heaven . . . right!)

In that hour Jesus rejoiced in the spirit, and said, I thank thee O Father, Lord of heaven and earth, that thou hast hid these things from the wise and prudent, and hast revealed them to babes: even so Father; for it seemed good in thy sight. (How mature could these 70 have been in Christ? They were babes in the faith).

All things are delivered to me of my Father: and no man knoweth who the Son is, but the Father; and who the Father is but the Son, and he to whom the Son will reveal Him."

Oh please, dear traditional friend, do not dismiss this; do not try to put in the restrictions of a Church doctrine. Receive this wonderful truth and be part of freeing God's people from bondage.

Have you ever considered Jesus' job description? Have you given much thought to what HE said He came to do? His anointing was spoken of by Isaiah, and received and confirmed, when Jesus stood in the little synagogue where it was his custom to worship in Nazareth. As a matter of fact, it is the event in Scripture that follows His water baptism and the Holy Spirit baptizing Him with power. After he trounced on Satan in the wilderness He returned to Nazareth, His hometown.

Jesus gave His job description. For maybe 25 years Jesus had been attending the synagogue, listening to the teachers. He listened and learned in silence. Worshiping and learning from the Rabbis, this day would be different. Today, Jesus would speak. Thirty years after He was prophetically born of a virgin, the Lord Jesus would speak. I can see the gentle, quiet Lord Jesus rise from his seat and call for the scrolls of Isaiah. What anointing and power must have come from His lips as He quoted from Isaiah's prophecy and He announced His job description.

"The Spirit of the Lord is upon me because He has anointed me to preach the gospel to the poor; the recovering of sight to the blind; to bind the brokenhearted, to preach deliverance to the captives, to set at liberty them that are bruised and to preach the acceptable year of the Lord." Luke 4:18.19

Amazing! The Bible declares that He closed the book and sat down.

What have we missed here? I don't hear this being proclaimed as the job of the Church, yet Jesus said in John 20:21, "As My Father has sent me, even so, send I you." Why is that not the job description of every pastor?

Our people not only need the gospel of salvation, but hearts are broken and need mending. Jesus came to bind, to heal, the broken hearted. People are sick and blind and He came to restore what the enemy has taken. People are bruised from life, some scarred since childhood. He was "bruised for our iniquities". . . that's why He can heal our bruises that came through iniquity. He came to break the bonds of captivity. Salvation is eternal, but it does not bring healing or break Satan's bonds. I honestly never understood this. Salvation was the only message I knew!

I discovered I had been living in only one room of a really big house. I camped out in the salvation room, I invited many people into that room and over the years more than 100,000 have joined me in that room. I really give praise to God for that! One day the Holy Spirit invited me to other parts of the house. I could hardly take in all that I saw as He took me to other rooms . . . one room right by the salvation room was the healing room. He anointed me to go into that room.

Oh, my goodness. I had believed that this room was closed, that it was no longer open. I saw in the hallway leading to this room many other rooms all with names of spiritual gifts. But I had always heard that these rooms were closed after the Bible was given to man. They told me not to even look for these rooms. Why did they do that? What man had told me was off limits, the Holy Spirit was now inviting me to . . . wow, I heard some rejoicing and praise coming from other rooms and this one, too, as God's People gave praise for various healings!

I saw the room where demons were being run off and I wanted in that room. People were in such peace and fulfillment as the robbers and thieves were being kicked out of their lives. It's a big house, I was discovering and I haven't been in all the rooms yet. Everything starts in the salvation room, but it leads to many other areas of the house. This is the way I felt when I began to see people healed and delivered. Why had I been so long in the salvation room? Because I didn't know the other rooms were open. . .I had believed a lie!

One of my mentors in deliverance ministry is Rev. Frank Hammond who wrote, among other books, *"PIGS IN THE PARLOR."* His ministry is called "CHILDREN'S BREAD." There is an account in Matthew 15 of a Syrophenecian woman, a Gentile coming to Jesus for help for her little girl who was "grieviously vexed with a devil." Jesus told her that He had come for the lost sheep of Israel. She was a Gentile therefore she did not qualify. She pleaded and Jesus said, "It is not right to take the children's bread and give it to the dogs (Gentiles)."

She was not one of the children of Israel. She was out of bounds. So desperate was she, that she fell at His feet and worshiped Him,

"Truth Lord, but even the dogs eat the crumbs that fall from the masters table."

Uh, oh! Now she had made a statement of faith and Jesus said, "O woman, great is your faith, be it unto you according as you will." Her faith got her in. She now qualified as one of the children, and she got what she came for.

What she came for was healing and deliverance . . . Jesus called it the Children's Bread! Another instance where Jesus slapped Satan on the way to the cross, was when a Gentile received salvation, healing and deliverance.

The fourth bad day was at the cross. Every drop of blood paid for something. Not only was salvation's work finished at the Cross, Satan was finished there also. The innocent spotless blood of Jesus that began to stream from the stripes on His back in the judgement hall was paying for our healing! The first drop of blood that oozed from the beating had sufficient power to bring healing to all suffering mankind. Prophecy was being fulfilled. While Satan thought he was having victory, his doom was being forever sealed.

Isaiah 53:5,6 says,

"But He was wounded for our transgressions, he was bruised for our iniquities: the chastisement of our peace was upon Him; and with His stripes we are healed. All we like sheep have gone astray; we have turned every one to his own way; and the Lord has laid on Him the iniquity of us all."

Wounded - for our transgressions!
Bruised - for our iniquities!
Chastised - for our peace!
Stripes - beaten for our healing!

Four separate things were paid for in this one verse. Sin, evil spirits, peace and healing. Satan did not even recognize that this was a bad day. He deceived himself. But the blood that was shed will never lose it's power! Never lose it's power to cover sin, to expose wickedness and darkness, to bring peace and to afford healing. Never lose its power.

The fourth bad day continues into the resurrection! No resurrection, no victory. If Christ be not risen, Paul says, "I am of all men most miserable." Oh, but he is risen indeed! Matthew 28:6 declares: "He is not here: for He is risen from the dead . . ." In Revelation 1:18 Jesus said, "I am He that liveth, and was dead; and, behold, I am alive for evermore, Amen; and have the keys of hell and of death." Every drop of Blood He shed at Calvary was crushing the serpent's head, every drop of Blood paid for something and gave us authority over the devil. A baaad day for the devil!

When Jesus descended into hell, he went to his house and beat him up again. I can also visualize this happening. Maybe the demons were having a party, celebrating the death of Jesus. Maybe there was a card table where Satan, Beelzebub, Abaddon and Belial were playing poker. The doorbell rings and Satan says, "Abaddon, get the door." I can see this ugly demon strolling to the door, somewhat cocky, he looks through the peephole and immediately passes out. He hits the floor with a thud! Beelzebub rises from his chair and says, "I'll get it." He goes to the door and as he glances through the little slit in the glass, he grabs his heart and starts stumbling and stammering. He can't speak. Satan jumps up in disgust and opens the door. There stands Jesus! "Oh no, no, No," cries Satan.

Jesus says, "I've come for the keys! Give me the keys." He punches him one more time. He took the keys from Satan and now He has the keys of hell and death. He ripped the stinger out of him taking away death's sting forever for those who believe, He jumped up and down on the grave robbing it of its victory and He is alive forever more. That was a baaad day for the devil!

The fifth bad day occurred only 50 days later. Jesus walked on the earth and showed Himself alive for forty days. The Church was told to go into all the world and preach the gospel, to cast out demons in His Name and to lay hands on the sick and they would be healed. . .but not to go until. . .until the power came.

They waited in prayer for ten days. Have you ever prayed and nothing happened? Keep praying until the answer comes! They prayed 1 day, then 2, then 3, 4, 5, 6, 7, 8, 9, and nothing happened. Nothing, do you suppose there was any talk of not continuing? Do you think maybe some suggested that they had prayed and tarried long enough. I feel certain that they did.

But on that 10th day. "*Suddenly there came a sound from heaven . . .*" Acts 1:8 & 2:1-4. The power came! When the power came, they were energized to fulfill the commission on their life. Now go, now preach, now witness. Multitudes began to accept Christ. The gospel was being spread all over and was being received all over. Jesus had already spoken, *"If I be lifted up, I will draw all men unto me."* I can see Satan tremble at another of his mistakes and must have said, *"Oh my, oh no, I had one Jesus to deal with, now I've got little Jesuses everywhere!"*

Christians were beginning to understand the principal of binding and loosing. The words that Jesus spoke were coming alive to them. "Behold, I give unto YOU POWER . . . OVER ALL THE POWER OF THE ENEMY." It is a bad day for the devil when that truth comes alive in believers today. Speak to those demons in the NAME OF JESUS. Tell the demons that you face; "You are defeated, I have victory in Christ Jesus. I am in Him and He is in me. And He that is within me is greater than he that is in the world. YOU back off; you are the one going to hell, not me. You are the one with a problem, not me, I have eternal life living in me, you have a bad future ahead of you and you and your principalities and powers are all under the feet of Jesus. You back off! Go in the Name of Jesus Christ. I overcome you by the Blood and the Power of His Name. I resist you, I rebuke you and you must be obedient!" We have been given power of attorney, use it. Do it, give him a bad day.

The sixth bad day is on the horizon. Revelation 20:1-3 tells us that he's got a couple of Bad Days coming too! Someday ONE angel will bind him for 1000 years and while Satan is bound, we will rule and reign with Jesus on this earth for a full one thousand years! That will be the 6th Bad day for the devil. Think about it One Holy Angel will bind him. "Is this the man?" Lies, deceits, threats. He has got some bad days coming. Remind him occasionally.

The seventh and final bad day is recorded in Revelation 20:7-10 The devil, the beast and the false prophet, the unholy trinity will be cast into the lake of fire and brimstone and shall be tormented day and night for ever and ever! He's got a BAAAD DAY coming. Every time he reminds you of your failures, your guilt, and your past...remind him of his future! Is this the man? Stand on the WORD, we have victory, he is defeated, Jesus has given us POWER over ALL THE POWER OF THE ENEMY! Praise God!

During the time Satan is bound for 1000 years we will rule and reign with Jesus on this earth. We who are saved, that is. If you are not saved, you have a bad day coming also; your fate will be the same as Satan's. But because he is defeated, you can have life everlasting through Christ Jesus. Believers have some great days ahead. A day when God Himself will wipe away all tears; there will be no more sorrow, heartache or pain, because the former things will be no more.

It is the former things that we deal with now.

Chapter 4

WHAT EXACTLY IS SCRIPTURAL DELIVERANCE?

Deliverance is probably not what you have heard that it is. It is not like the movies. It is not like Hollywood; it is like the **Holy Word**! It is for believers! It is nothing to be afraid of, and is totally non-threatening to the individual. It is simply inner healing by removal of the cause of the problem. . .remember the verse that we used to open this book. Acts 10:38 says that *"How that God anointed Jesus of Nazareth with the Holy Ghost and with power: who went about doing good, and healing all that were oppressed of the devil."* That is what deliverance is, breaking the oppressing power of the enemy!

Why could Jesus do all that He did? The simple answer is that He was God's Son sent into this world to do all that He did. God sent Him with power and authority, right? God gave Him authority and Jesus gave us authority. Scriptural deliverance is relieving spiritual oppression!

Dr. Charles Stanley says that, in a sense, demons can possess areas of a Christian's life, that is, once they are in the soul and flesh they can control areas not submitted to the Holy Spirit. Complete possession of a believer is not possible, because the Holy Spirit lives in our spirit, that part of us which is eternal.

Is it correct to say that deliverance ministers are exorcists? In the proper definition of the word, yes. The goal of the deliverance minister is to expel the demon from the soul and flesh of the individual, however, it is not like the movies and the media have depicted exorcism. It often occurs without any significant manifestation and is completely non-threatening to the one receiving the ministry of deliverance. It is not much more than praying for the individual in terms of what goes on. The "deliverance dramas" are rare, though they do happen.

The most common misconception I encounter is that only evil people have demons. Somewhere in church history the notion was presented that Christians could not have demons. Nothing could be further from the truth! If you are alive . . . you are a candidate.

The average believer has either been taught or has come to a "logical" conclusion, that demons and the Holy Spirit can not co-exist in the same body. That's what most people struggle with.

Demons take up residence in the body and the soul, but not in the spirit. The Holy Spirit abides in the spirit of a believer. If you have believed this, because of a "logical" conclusion, then you must account for how sin dwells in a person where the Holy Spirit abides. How does evil manifest in believers, if we use that logic? Where does the anger, hatred and bitterness live? Where does lust manifest, if not in the body? It is a foolish conclusion. Demons can and do live in believers, if they have been granted legal permission.

A second mistake I see when the word deliverance is mentioned is that <u>people want to think "demon possession"</u>. . . it is NOT possession. Possession implies ownership, we are owned by the Lord Jesus! We are purchased, redeemed, bought with a price. We are possessed by the Holy Spirit of God, who lives in our Spirit. Oppression takes place in the soul and in the flesh. The soul is the area of torment. . .mind, will, emotions. . . and that is where the demons do their misdeeds. This is the warfare that Paul so often talks about. David in Psalms 116 describes oppression and deliverance perfectly. David said, *"the pains of hell got hold on me . . . I found trouble and sorrow . . . He loosed my bonds."*

<u>Demons must have legal rights</u> to one's life. They cannot intrude at will. It always involves legal consent from either the individual or from God. Generational curse, of course, does not involve our will, but does grant permission to evil spirits through the sins of the fathers, (mothers), for three to four generations. Meaning ANYONE born could be born with a spirit that has legal right according to Exodus 20:5. This is the most common entryway for demon spirits, and to think it could not happen to you is evidence of the power of their deception.

Entryways, many times are there, not because of sin committed, but because of things that happened. Trauma is a very common doorway. To believe that torment is sent by God is borderline blasphemy. God sends good and perfect gifts. Demons are tormentors. Coming to a scriptural understanding of this is the first step toward release.

Demons, evil spirits, unclean spirits, devils, spirits of infirmity, principalities, powers etc., <u>must have PERMISSION</u> to be in someone's life. Jesus had to have permission to be in your life. God requires our permission. Jesus says in Revelation 3:20 that *"He stands at the door and knocks . . ."* Why does He knock at our door? He must have our permission to enter our lives!

Demons or evil spirits must also have our consent, and permission is granted in many ways through each person's life. The Holy Spirit honors our will, demons must also, and cannot intrude without some kind of consent. (Consent can be as simple as being in the presence of a Ouija Board, a childhood abuse or trauma, periods of anger or unforgiveness etc). When people come to me for deliverance I ask them to complete a questionnaire. The questions came after years of deliverance experience and noticing common doorways for spirits. I ask people to pray after completing the form that I give them and ask the Holy Spirit to bring to their remembrance anything that may have given access to the demon powers.

Once consent is granted the demon takes up residence in the soul or flesh and begins to <u>build a "kingdom" bent on destruction.</u> Jesus described the works of Satan as to <u>"rob, kill, steal, destroy."</u> I have yet to locate a demon power with any other function. Now, the oppression begins, because the demon has been granted permission to be there.

Part of the deliverance process is to determine what doorways or entryways were granted to evil spirits. That is, what permission or consent, do the demons have to BE THERE. The fact that they are there, indicates they had consent. The question now is, do they have permission to stay?

You may wonder what would give a demon legal consent to stay in a believers life. Consent to stay could be, for example, unforgiveness in one's life, that is God-given permission for demons to torment. Matthew 18:23-35. If unforgiveness is in a believer's life, demons do not have to leave! They have God's permission to STAY . . . and permission to torment. Another example of permission to stay would be sin in individuals lives that they are un-willing to surrender to the Lord. That will block a deliver-ance, because the demon has a legal right to stay.

The bottom line is "permission to stay." If all consent to be there-stay there is canceled, then the demons must be obedient to the command in the Name of Jesus Christ to leave.

Deliverance cannot take place against someone's will and can even involve more than just their willingness to be free, often it requires a desire to be free.

Demon spirits are very organized and are hierarchy ori-ented. They are very structured and you might view their kingdom as having a CEO with vice-presidents, managers, supervisors and workers. Or maybe a better description would be a military pecking order. There will be a "boss" who runs everything. They like to be called "princes." The Prince may have several princes under him, who all have varied functions intent on the believers demise and de-struction. But, every one will bow at the Name of Jesus Christ. You need not fear.

That Satan has a demonic hierarchy is well documented in Scripture. Ephesians 6 tells us that, ". . . we wrestle not with flesh and blood, but against principalities, against powers, against the rulers of darkness of this world, against spiritual wickedness in high places." From

Satan's throne or his place of rule, there is a vast kingdom of darkness. I don't know the layers of authority in this kingdom. I can only speculate how many demon powers separate Satan from the attacks on my life. I would guess there are several in the chain of command. I remember an inmate came up to me after a recent service in a Texas prison. He said, *"Sir, the Holy Spirit told me to tell you that Satan has assigned a high-ranking spirit to you. Do you know what that means?"* Yes, I knew. Before I could even allow fear a place in my heart, the Holy Spirit spoke to me, *"Same authority, you have the same authority in Jesus' Name. Just keep walking!"*

High-ranking spirit? There are many in the heavenlies. I do not believe we have been given authority to challenge these demon powers. Our authority is on this earth as it has to do with mankind. My authority, I believe, is restricted to what is mine, and to where I am, and to whomsoever comes willing under my authority. To tear down heavenly positions of darkness, I believe, can be very dangerous and foolish. I have seen many come under attacks of sickness and family trauma because of unwise ventures into warfare.

Stepping outside our realm of authority is a mistake. Challenging demons is a mistake. Knowing our bound-aries and limitations is a must in spiritual warfare. As it has to do with me, my family, my "stuff". . . Jesus Christ has given me full authority over all the power of the enemy. As it has to do with "powers in the heavenlies" I believe that battle is won in intercession. That is where the angels fight in our behalf. Repentance and confession of ancestral wrongs lends strength in that battle. I would guess a spiritual hierarchy would break down similar to the following:

<u>**Satan-Beast-Fasle Prophet**</u> *(Lucifer)*
<u>**Beelzebub**</u>*-the world is mine Prince of Demons*
<u>**Abadoddon-Apollyon**</u> *King of bottomless pit demons*
<u>**Xanthan**</u> *- claims totality including universe*
point is that we do not deal directly with Satan, but with
<u>**Baphomet**</u>　　　　<u>**Samhain**</u>　　　　　　<u>***Others***</u>
<u>**Ma Ha Bone**</u> *(Prince of all Free Masonry spirits) -* <u>**Moletha**</u>-
(witchcraft/voodoo) etc.
<u>**Witchcraft - Sickness/Disease - Calamity - Distress -**</u>
<u>**Poverty -Lust -Other**</u>
<u>**Territorial spirits**</u> *- continents and nations*
Example: **Adirondack** *- North America*
Example: <u>**"Nemtalia"**</u> *Egypt*
<u>**District spirits**</u> *- Example:*<u>**"Elamond"**</u>
Colorado, Oklahoma, Kansas, Missouri, New Mexico and
parts of Texas
<u>**Regional spirits**</u>
Example: "<u>**Singfa"**</u> *Southern Oklahoma*
<u>**Counties**</u> *- Sections*
Example: "<u>**Ahmigihad"**</u> *Carter County, Oklahoma*
Example: "<u>**Oncar"**</u> *Estes County, Colorado*
<u>**Cities**</u>
Example: "<u>**Cameron"**</u> *Fort Worth, TX*
<u>**Communities**</u>
Example:<u>**False religion**</u>
Harassing-hindering-blocking-temptation-
blindness (spiritual)-Floaters-Roaming spirits
<u>**Individual kingdom princes**</u>
Example: <u>**Fear**</u>
Examples: <u>**Darkness Spirits**</u>

This is just an "opinion" of how the kingdom might break down, it is likely much more sophisticated. My guess is that there would be many more levels of authority. It is his underlings, the demon powers that we confront are probably those with the least demonic power. The demonic kingdom established within an individual is generally on assignment from an outside spirit of higher rank. An example would be that of a person who has demons there by permission of generational curse from Masonic ancestry. The prince of that kingdom would likely report to Ma Ha Bone. I have found this to be a high ranking "Masonry" spirit.

The assignments can be anything from *"stealing joy"* to *"murder or premature death."* Remember, their goal is that of Satan, *"rob, kill, steal, destroy."* I have found the kingdoms established within people to be extremely consistent. There is little variation in the structure of the kingdom. The demons seem not be very creative or ingenious. The pattern is virtually always the same.

Some of the demons in the internal kingdom are assigned the duty of *"gatekeeper"* and it is their function to bring other demons in at every opportunity. In the process of deliverance I will address these spirits and command that when they leave, that every gate is closed and locked!

A typical deliverance session, if there is such a thing, can vary in length from one hour to many hours, but generally can be accomplished in a couple of hours. The more prepared the individual is, the smoother the process . . . with some exceptions. I always remind the candidate that the process is not a ritual and it is permissible to ask questions, pause for a restroom break or a drink of water. The deliverance setting is casual, yet, it is Holy. We always depend upon the Holy Presence of God's Spirit to lead us and guide us. Deliverance is a truth encounter . . . it is not a power encounter!

Demons are all liars and they will submit to the truth of the Word of God and the Powerful Name of Jesus Christ. Demons, totally understand the battle, they know they are defeated and know they must be obedient to the commands of the Lord Jesus. They will bow their knee and they will leave, when they are commanded to leave! It is not un-common for the person seeking deliverance to experience manifestations of the evil spirits, prior to the session; as well as during the session. They may become extremely nervous (the demons), because they know their time is short. They will attempt to frighten the person or plant lies of destruction they (the demons) may do. It is also common to have nightmares or to experience sick-ness. Demons may also confuse or disorient the individual.

A Methodist pastor came to me for ministry. He had been a missionary for a few years in Haiti. He was certain that he had "picked up" some evils spirits while there. He was right! He told me he became nauseated from the moment he contacted me. He called me on his cell phone as he was driving to my office. The pastor said, "I am on the Airport Freeway and I know exactly where your office is . . . but I have become so disoriented that you are going to have to direct me there."

When the pastor arrived, he even looked sick. He said, "Is it normal for me to be seeing demons at this time." I as-sured him that nothing was normal, but that I had not en-countered this before. "What are you seeing?" I asked. "I see one large demon standing between you and me and I see two on my back." He felt like he was getting very ill. I immediately bound the spirits and started the deliverance. He was delivered of many evil spirits and some of them had come to him, when he ministered in Haiti. He also had many spirits by permission of freemasonry in his ancestry. There was a strong occult kingdom established. However, it was crushed in the Name of Jesus Christ and the pastor is now free.

The demons may attack the individuals minds to make them think they must be crazy, if they really think demons are the problem. They may "tell" the individuals that the deliverance minister is a "jerk" that he doesn't know what he is doing, that this will not work, etc. All of these things are common and it is an attempt to keep the person in bondage. The truth is, the demons know how all of this works. They know much better than we do. They become very nervous, when they know they are going to be confronted in the Name of Jesus.

WHERE DO DEMONS LIVE IN A BELIEVER?

Jesus said, *"out of your belly shall flow rivers of living water . . . this spake He of the Spirit . . ."* John 7:38,39. He is talking about the Holy Spirit of God. However, it seems the belly, the mid-section is also the seat of the evil spirits. It is very common for them to manifest in this area with a stirring or discomfort in the stomach. This is most common. Headaches are very common occurrences prior to, and during deliverance. Demon spirits also live in the central nervous system, this is their control center. Numbness, tingling and dizziness are also very common when the demons are aroused. I always tell those who are candidates for deliverance to not be alarmed, they will not harm you! Just know these are very common symptoms. I have seen literally thousands of deliverances and rarely are there not some of these conditions present.

When demons inhabit a believer, they dwell in the "body" and the "soul." I once encountered a spirit and commanded the spirit to reveal where he was (in the person). He responded with, "*In the mind.*" I said, "So you are in the brain?" With a measure of frustration in the response, the spirit, speaking through the individual, said. "*NO! I'm in the mind.*" The mind is part of the soul, the brain is part of the body. The *mind, will* and *emotions* make up the soul. The only way a demon could enter the spirit of a man would be if the person was lost. This would clearly be, demonic possession.

When the demons are expelled, commanded to leave, they most often come out on the individual's breath. Sometimes with a deep sigh, a cough, a yawn, a burp . . . occasionally, some gagging, but they will come out and they must be obedient. I have "witnessed" many types of releases. Some say, "They are leaving out the pores of my skin. I feel them coming out of the top of my head." "My fingers got very hot and then I sensed them leave through the tips of my fingers." Some say, "I see them leaving like a flock of birds." The candidate always knows when the demons leave. They cannot be disobedient to the command of the Lord Jesus.

When the demons leave I always command them to go into the abyss never to return. I will discuss this later. I also command that they cannot harm the individual, nor can they leave you and go into someone else. Often the individual may hear the demons saying in his mind . . . "I'll leave, but I'll go to your kids . . . etc." I remind everyone to not be alarmed by their threats, they will do as they are commanded . . . period!

Generally, the candidates will "hear" the demon's response in their minds, and report to me what they have heard. . .sometimes they may "see" something, when the demons are commanded to obey the Holy Spirit and Holy Angels force them to obedience.

For example: Jesus spoke to the demoniac in Gadera (Mark 5) and said, *"What is your name?"* The demons in the man responded, *"Legion, because we are many."* The demons always respond. I command, always in the Name of Jesus Christ, the prince demon to reveal his identity either by name or function. The deliverance candidate will immediately get a response in their mind. . .I ask them to report what they hear or see.

The names will be very unusual, sometimes names that will surprise the individual, most common is that the demon will reveal his function, i.e., FEAR, DOUBT, HATRED, etc. It is really not complicated. Once the demon is identified, there is just one question, "Do you have consent from Jehovah God to stay?" It is over at that point, if the spirit does not have consent, he will be commanded to go to the abyss and he will!

At this point in the deliverance we will have canceled all permissions for demons to stay. This is done in the beginning and will be discussed later.

There can be any number of demons present and the number is not significant. Every demon power will bow at the Name of Jesus Christ!
Now, I don't know how many deliverance ministers there

are. But that's how many varied opinions there are about the correct way to minister deliverance. Some say don't speak to the demons, or don't allow the demons to talk, and they are very successful ministers. Many say do it all by discernment calling the spirits out as the Holy Spirit reveals them to you. I do not disagree with this method, but I have found it to be ineffective and thus incomplete in my ministry.

Others say to put the demons under oath before Jehovah God and command them to obey, to reveal how many are present, what their function or assignment is and then to cancel that in the Name of Jesus Christ and command the spirits to the abyss and to never return in Jesus Name. I have found this to be most successful in my ministry.

Some scoff and say, "Don't interview the demons, just command them to go." My personal experience, first of all, is that it is not an interview, it is breaking their permission to be in one's life. It is not conversation, it is CONFRONTATION! If a demon has consent to stay . . . from Jehovah God (curse-disobedience, etc.) or from the individual (unconfessed sin or unwillingness to repent) then the demons do not have to leave, no matter who is giving the command, or how many times it is given. The permission to be there must be canceled or the demons will not leave. Perhaps they will leave when commanded, but if doorways are not closed, then other demons can enter.

There is not a "correct" way spelled out in Scripture. Jesus certainly spoke to the demons and demanded a name. That is clear. There was also conversation recorded in the Mark 5 encounter. That was my first reference when I was faced with deliverance, what did Jesus do? There certainly are other instances where Jesus commanded demons to not speak, however this was in the Temple and the demon was trying to expose Jesus. This is how God has shown me to do it, and with the Holy Spirit's help I have been very successful at seeing folks delivered and healed.

PREPARATION FOR DELIVERANCE

DELIVERANCE CANDIDATE:

1. Make sure that you are sincere; be open, be honest, don't hold back.

2. Desire to be free so that you can serve the Lord.

3. Ask the Holy Spirit to reveal areas of demonic bondage or torment.

4. Look over your life (and ancestry) to discover possible doorways

5. Determine to be free, no matter what grip the demons may have (addictions etc.).

6. Don't be intimidated by "what others may think."

7. Associate deliverance with Jesus and freedom, rather than demons and bondage.

8. While your faith is not the key . . . exercise your faith as much as possible.

9. View this as part of God's gift to us in Jesus Christ.
10. Know this may be the beginning of freedom for your

family and offspring.

DELIVERANCE MINSTER:

1. Make sure my life is clean and that the Holy Spirit has reign in my life.

2. Gather all the information possible from the individual concerning possible doorways in their life, this of course, includes generational information and possible curses.

3. Make the individual comfortable and make certain they understand that this is an act of love.

4. Lead them through prayers of renunciation, breaking of soul ties, repentance, confessing that they are born again, that Jesus is Savior, Lord, Deliverer, Healer and that He has broken the power of curse. Have them confess that they truly desire to be free.

5. Bind the demon powers according to Scripture in Jesus Christ's Name.

6. Command the prince, the boss of the kingdom, to identify himself by name or function.

7. Determine if any spirit present has consent to stay. (If yes, command that the consent be revealed and then lead the individual to pray/confess to cancel that consent).

8. Command the spirits to become one spirit, with no passing on of duties, and as one spirit to leave the

individual, go into the abyss and never return.

9. Go back and check . . . maybe two or three times, make sure nothing is left.

10. Pray anointing and protection for the individual and put something in their hands to help them to walk in continued freedom.

For the deliverance minister, I believe the most important thing he should remember is, John 15:5

"*. . . Without me you can do nothing.*"

I tell every candidate, "Expect to be free!"

Chapter 5

WHAT IS THE CORRECT TERMINOLOGY?

The King James Bible, as well as most other translations, uses the word "possessed" when talking about demons in people. However, that is not the meaning of the Greek word translated "possessed" in the Bible. The Greek word *"daimonizomai"* would be better translated "demonized." It means to "be under the influence of demons," to "be affected by demons," or to "have demons." There are very few people who are totally owned, or possessed by demons. Obviously a Christian cannot be "possessed" by a demon, because Christians belong to God through the Blood of Jesus Christ. Ownership is implied in the word "possession." Believers are owned by the Lord Jesus. They have been purchased, bought with a price, by the shed Blood of Jesus. The question is can Christians have demons. . .the answer is yes! What does the Bible say?

Ephesians 2:2 says that demons are at work in the sons of disobedience. Disobedience certainly grants permission to evil spirits. The truth is, people who are disobeying God are giving evil spirits a right to work, not only around them, but also in them. Peter declared that Satan had filled the heart of Ananias. "Filled the heart" implies access to the body and soul through disobedience. Doesn't that indicate that anyone who lies (one of the sins we seem to classify as a small one), could have their heart filled by Satan, or more correctly by one of his demon spirits.

Paul told the believers in Ephesus: "Neither give place to the devil" (Ephesians 4:27). This implies that it is possible for a Christian to give a place to the devil, or to his demons. The place given in this verse is by not confessing the sin and allowing it to linger. If a person has given space, or a place, to demons by their own choices, they are in need of deliverance.

Correct terminology for a believer with demons is probably "demonized." However, "oppression" is also scripturally correct. Acts 10:38-43 is a great section of Scripture to describe scriptural deliverance. In Peter's sermon at Caesarea he is talking about the Son of God that had been rejected, but now has risen from the dead. Peter is preaching about a Saving, Delivering, Healing Jesus. He is describing the ministry of The Anointed One sent from God and the One Whom he served.

"How God anointed Jesus of Nazareth with the Holy Ghost and with power: Who went about doing good, and healing all that were oppressed of the devil; for God was with Him . . . and He commanded us to preach unto the people, and to testify that it is He which was ordained of God to be the judge of the quick and the dead. To Him give all the prophets witness, that through His name whosoever believeth in Him shall receive remission of sins."

Jesus went about doing good and HEALING ALL THEM THAT WERE OPPRESSED OF THE DEVIL. Deliverance in it's truest sense is oppression healing. It is removal of the oppressive source, and release from the consequences of demonic presence.

The word exorcism is certainly frightening to folks today, because of the misuse and abuse of the word. Obviously the movie, "The Exorcist," has left a lasting negative impression on the public. However, the word is correct terminology in that it speaks of "expelling demon powers." Deliverance is probably the second most "frightening" term to use when describing the process but it is the word Jesus used in Luke 4:18. *"He has sent me to preach deliverance to the captives . . ."* The prophetic word from Isaiah 61:1 is *"To proclaim liberty"* . . . that is what deliverance is! It is freedom from the presence of demon powers that abide in the soul or flesh, or that are attached to a believer's life.

WHAT ABOUT THEM RETURNING IN GREATER NUMBERS AND STRENGTH?

"When an unclean spirit goes out of a man, he goes through dry places, seeking rest, and finds none. Then he says, 'I will return to MY HOUSE from which I came.' And when he comes, he finds it EMPTY, swept, and put in order. Then he goes out and takes with him seven other spirits more wicked than himself, and they enter and dwell there, and the last state of that man is worse than the first." (Matthew 12:43- 45) (Emphasis mine)

This passage of Scripture has caused great concern for those who contemplate deliverance. It has always been interpreted that when evil spirits have been CAST out of someone, that they have the option to someday return. I don't believe that is what this verse indicates. My personal experience is that I have never seen this happen, and I don't believe this is an option. Demonic invasion by other spirits is certainly possible, if the individual opens doorways through disobedience. That is possible whether demon spirits have been cast out or not.

This Scripture says that "when the unclean spirit is <u>gone</u> out," but it does not say why he has gone out. It seems to me that the spirit here has left on his own volition. Maybe he left, because 'his house' was spiritually clean and he found it very uncomfortable. In every translation the word "gone" means to leave by one's own volition. He must have had permission to be there, else he could not be there, that is a scriptural given. There is no indication that this permission had been canceled. The doorway by which this demon spirit left would still be open, if he chose to return.

Maybe he thought he would find a better house. Whatever the reason for leaving, he decides to return and check out the situation. Now look how he found the house . . . "empty, swept and put in order." This does not indicate to me that the spirit had permission, because of re-opened doors. The house was clean and in order. What seems obvious to me is that the demon had permission through a previous doorway that had never been closed. An empty house is not permission for demons to enter a believer. An unclean house is permission. This house was clean and swept . . . and decorated.

There have been volumes written about filling the house with the Holy Spirit and with the Holy Word to keep the cast out spirits, from returning. That is not suggested here. Obviously, the Holy Spirit should be welcomed. He should be invited to fill every void that was once occupied by demonic spirits. But, the Holy Spirit does not keep demon spirits out, **we do** by obedience and confession of sin, by not believing the lie. The Word of God will not keep demons out, if there is an open doorway.

For instance, you can read the Word, memorize it, teach it, quote it, love it, share it and still, by having unconfessed sin in your life, open a door to demons. You can be bathed in the Holy Spirit and carry unforgiveness in your life and God will turn you over to the tormentors. So the point of the story that Jesus shares in Matthew 12 seems to be that, if there is a doorway, (portal, gate, or legal right), the demon can leave by his own choice and, if the doorway by which he left is not closed, he can return and bring others with him. This is how kingdoms are established anyway, by bringing others in.

I believe the Scripture teaches that when demons have been expelled by the authority of the Name of Jesus Christ that returning to that person is not an option. In one case Jesus made that clear when He said, *"Enter her no more."* I personally believe they are to go into the abyss and are taken out of circulation, until they are released during the tribulation period. I have found that the demons will bring to the mind of the deliverance candidate the "possibility" that they may return. Often the lie is that they will come back in greater force. Some are frightened to the point that they are not certain they want to go through with deliverance. There has been great misuse of the above Scripture.

Chapter 6

WHERE DO THE DEMONS GO?

Let me repeat something I said earlier. I don't have all the answers and I certainly can't guarantee that demons must go into the abyss. However, since I have been given authority in Jesus Name to cast them out, I also give them specific instructions on what they can and cannot do. I command that they cannot leave and go to someone else and that they cannot pass their duties on to other demons. If we are just freeing one person so that the demons may go find another person, it seems contradictory to all that Jesus came to do.

Some ministers are very certain that their way of performing the deliverance process is the only way. Some are very dogmatic on where the demons are commanded to go. One will say, "They must go to the feet of Jesus to be judged by Him and then sent where He determines." I say, "They have already been to the feet of Jesus, they are now under His feet!" I believe the authority he gives us to cast them out includes telling them where to go. Have you ever wanted to tell a demon where to go?

Others will say they should be banished to "dry places." I have never understood this, the Scripture clearly says that those in dry places have the option to return. The abyss seemed to be the understood place where demons would go when Jesus cast them out. I command demons to go not just "to" the abyss, but "into" the abyss. They are such legalist that I try not to give them any loopholes.

Generally, demons won't stay in anyone, who consistently submits to God and resists the devil. (James 4:7). The devil and all demons must flee from such a person, (submitted to God), when they are resisted in the Name of Jesus Christ. Submitting to God in this way is to not grieve the Holy Spirit (Ephesians 4:30). It is certainly clear that as believers we can "grieve the Holy Spirit," and that we can "quench" the Holy Spirit. But, as we are submitted to God, it is then that we please the Holy Spirit. Remember demons MUST have consent to torment believers. When all consent is canceled and demon powers have been commanded to leave in Jesus Christ's Name, demons have no choice, but to obey.

Can I tell you for certain where demons go? No, but I can with some degree of certainty. After each demon is expelled in the Name of Jesus Christ, I always command a remaining spirit to reveal where that spirit is. The command is that the demon go immediately and directly into the abyss. When the remaining spirit is put under oath before Jehovah God, they will confess that the expelled spirit is in the abyss.

There was a time when my command was simply "come out immediately and go to the abyss." Again, I learned that the demons are such legalists and masters of deceit that they would go to the abyss, but not *into* it. It was like telling them to go to the house, instead of telling them to go into the house. I found when they would do this that often they did return, some times they would come back before the deliverance session was over.

My experience has been that once they are in the abyss with the command to never return that they are taken out of circulation. I do not get too caught up in this, because there is no genuine way of knowing. Jesus certainly did command spirits to "enter no more."

I know of one deliverance ministry that commands spirits go to dry and barren places. This, of course, is because of the reference in Matthew 12:43, but is not an accurate interpretation of Scripture. And, even if it was, it is clear that, when demons are in "dry places," they are able to return.

Other ministries believe that we do not have authority to command demons into the abyss. Their thinking is that this amounts to judgement upon the demon spirits and that right belongs to Jesus Christ alone. People in this camp often command the spirits to go to the feet of Jesus, so Jesus can judge then and send them where He determines. I respect this viewpoint, but believe it is also incorrect. The demons have already been to the feet of Jesus and they have already been judged by Him. He trampled on them at Calvary and has already put all things under his feet! Ephesians 1:22.

There have been occasions when I have a demon power bound and ready to be cast out, that I have given the demon a choice of where he wants to go; to the feet of Jesus or into the abyss. I would say that 9 out of 10 times he chooses the feet of Jesus. This in itself is not conclusive.

I am aware that all demons are liars, but you do get a measure of truth when the demon power is commanded to speak truth before Jehovah God. Demons do not like to be brought before God's throne and commanded to speak truth. They get very angry. Truth greatly disturbs demon powers.

I suppose there are enough demons that sending a couple of hundred into the abyss does not greatly impact their affect on humanity. One thing we can be certain of is that Satan was only able to recruit a third of the heavenly host. There will always be twice as many holy angels as there are demon powers. The Bible calls demons powers Satan's angels, *"Then shall he say unto them on the left hand, Depart from me, ye cursed, into everlasting fire, prepared for the devil and his angels."* Matthew 25:41

We do know the final abode for demon spirits will be into everlasting fire. They will be cast along with Satan, the Beast and the False Prophet into the lake of fire. Revelation 20:10.

We also know that there are demons already in the abyss according to Revelation chapter 9. These demons will not be released, until the tribulation period. I believe this is where demon spirits should be sent today. I also believe Jesus gave us the authority to do so. To me, it makes no sense to simply command a spirit to leave. What's the purpose, if that spirit can then go to someone else or perhaps return.

I deal with these creatures of evil with a measure of finality! I believe that is what Jesus did, and I believe that demons understand that the abyss is where they are to go. I don't give them any breaks and try not to leave any loop holes.

Chapter 7

AUDIENCE OR ARMY?

WHAT HAPPENS WHEN THIS IS NOT TAUGHT IN OUR PULPITS AND BIBLE STUDIES?

There is gross ignorance of demons as it relates to Christians. Why is there so much ignorance in the Body of Christ about spiritual warfare? I had a pastor and his wife in my office recently. He had brought a member of his congregation to see me. He could not bring freedom to the man through wise counsel and scriptural encouragement. After the deliverance session was over and the man had been freed of many demonic spirits, the pastor and his wife asked to stay and visit a while.

They had many questions. The pastor's wife was almost angry that she had not been taught about this. "Why is this not being taught?" She questioned, "Why has this been kept from us?" The pastor who had just finished his seminary training posed much of the same type questioning. "I have not heard one word about deliverance in my three years of schooling. I knew it was real. I knew from experience that demons were active in the lives of believers, but I am ignorant of this process I just witnessed. I want to know how to do this." They had seen firsthand a member of their congregation set free. The man was in deep depression and was suicidal. He had spirits of *rejection,* and *doubt*, *fear* tormented him. But not any more, he is free. The pastor asked if he could come and sit in on some deliverances, so he could teach his people how to be free and so

69

that he could "proclaim liberty to the captives."

Because this message, for the most part, has been omitted from the pulpit there is an anemic church in bondage to the enemy and the church is living beneath the oppressing power of the enemy. There will be great accountability for pastors, who refuse to preach this truth. The blame for an anemic, powerless, sickly church can be nowhere, but at the feet of the pastors. Like it or not, that is the truth!

BUILDING AUDIENCES INSTEAD OF ARMIES

I believe focus is the issue. Fear is a consideration. And faith is the missing ingredient. What do I mean by that? The focus of most churches seems to be in building an AUDIENCE, instead of an ARMY. A large audience seems to make everyone happy, pastors, deacons, finance committees etc. We all go home and say wow! But maybe we should look closer, maybe it should be "whoa" that we are saying. Aren't we supposed to be building soldiers, equipping them for battle? How can we build an army, when the church is not aware of the reality of the enemy?

The focus is wrong. The main objective is out of focus. Somewhere along the way we dropped an important part of the gospel message. I will tell you without blinking, or without consideration of backing up, that the average local church has so limited the work of the Holy Spirit that it is virtually impossible for God to bless what we do! This is sad! This must be corrected.

DIDN'T GOD SAY IT?

If what Jesus said about Himself is true, if the job description He gave for Himself is true, then we have fallen short of being like Him and presenting Him in the pulpit. Did

He come to seek and to save that which is lost? Absolutely! We do a pretty good job of presenting this Jesus. Did He say; Go into all the world and preach the gospel, baptizing in the Name of the Father, the Son and the Holy Spirit? Of course, He did and we do a good job of that. But what about the other things He said that we have virtually ignored? What about that?

Didn't He say, *"The Spirit of the Lord is upon me, because He has anointed me to preach the gospel to the poor; He has sent me to heal the brokenhearted, to preach deliverance to the captives, and the recovering of sight to the blind, to set at liberty them that are bruised, to preach the acceptable year of the Lord."* Are those not the words of our Lord Jesus, when he announced His ministry purpose? Absolutely they are! Did He not also say, *"As the Father has sent me, even so send I you."* John 20:21

Let's look and see if we are ministering as Jesus said He had come to minister. **Are we preaching the gospel to the poor?** Does the prosperity gospel work in the ghetto? Maybe we are doing a fair job of presenting the good news of Jesus Christ to the poor. I'll let you make your own conclusion here. But it seems in our AUDIENCE driven churches that the poor are not the focus of our desired audience. We generally want people who are most like us. **Are we healing the brokenhearted?** I'll tell you that this can't be done with an audience, it takes an ARMY. Broken hearts are all about us, the sweet Lord Jesus proclaimed this as part of His mission. Is the broken heart being ministered to in your church, do messages from your pulpit do anything to mend and bind broken hearts? Doesn't this require an arm around your brother. Doesn't this require compassion from individuals? Does it not include action on our part?

71

It requires that and it requires more. It involves an ARMY that will come against the demonic forces with the authority of the Name of Jesus Christ and in the power of His shed Blood. Pastors must teach every believer, and must be an example of the authority and power. We don't back up, we don't back down, we come against the very gates of hell in the mighty Name of Jesus Christ. We don't fear the enemy, because we know who we are and what Christ has given us. We look demon powers in the eye and command that they retreat!

Are we preaching deliverance to the captives? I know this will strike a nerve in many a pastor's heart. Are you even mentioning the word deliverance? Does that frighten you, and are you fearful of your members' reactions? Are you a little fearful that some may leave or become very uncomfortable? What about your seminary connections, is there some fear here as well? Denominational standing, is that an issue? Is retirement funding an issue? Withdrawing fellowship from your circle of denominational acquaintances? What is keeping you from preaching deliverance to the captives? Pastors, if you are curious whom in your church has demons, just preach about them, and you'll find out. They'll be knocking on your door and demanding no more preaching about such nonsense.

Could it be that you have really bought into the lie that demons no longer exist? Where did they go? I heard a foolish pastor say that "demons" were just really mental problems that people had, but because the people in Jesus' time on earth believed they actually were evil spirits that He spoke to them on their level of understanding. I believe this ignorance is borderline blasphemy.

Could you possibly believe that demonic spirits do not exist? If you do, then you are the most deceived of all and you have chosen not to believe the Word of God. Plain and simple you have denied Scripture! I want you to deal with the issue for your sake and for the sake of your people. Demonic bondage for believers is a reality! I believe the day is coming and I believe it will be very soon, that every pastor in every church will be faced with people in their congregation crying desperately to be free. I believe every pastor should go through deliverance and should prepare himself for the warfare that is going to intensify. Already, pastors, your people are in bondage.

Let me just add that I am a member of a very large Baptist Church, I am not on staff, I direct DON DICKERMAN MINISTRIES to prisons and to healing and deliverance needs. I have ministered deliverance to more than 100 members of this congregation including deacons, Sunday school teachers, musicians, singers, moms, dads and children. This is NOT the exception, it is the rule! Good people, God's people, are being held captive by Satan's kingdom of darkness and it is very real! Pastors, you must be obedient to the Holy Spirit regardless of the denominational pressures. You must.

I cannot help but ask WHY is this omitted from the gospel, not being taught in the seminaries and in the pulpits? My only conclusion is the FOCUS is wrong . . . we don't need an AUDIENCE, we need an ARMY. FEAR can no longer control the pastor's preaching. And FAITH must be placed in the Holy Word of God. God will honor the pure preaching and teaching of the Word. There is a great need today for a church with balance. Balance in the WORD and the SPIRIT. In one body there is great emphasis on the Word, but little dependance upon the Spirit. In another there is focus on the gifts and workings of the Holy Spirit, but little emphasis on the Word. God will bless the pastor who sees that there is proper balance and the people of that church will become an ARMY.

Are we preaching recovering of sight to the blind?
When is the last time you heard your preacher talk to you
about the healing mercies of the Lord Jesus? Pastor why
are you not laying hands on the sick and expecting them to
be healed? Why are you not teaching your people who are
sick to call for the elders of the church to let them pray
over them, anointing them with oil in the name of the Lord?

Do you not believe that the prayer of faith will bring healing to the sick? Are you afraid it might not happen? Fearful of being embarrassed? If you are not doing it, you are
not preaching the gospel, and you are not being obedient
to the call on your life.

I ask you to consider this? What pastor has not opened his
Bible to John 14 at a funeral and read the powerful words
of Jesus for comfort and hope? This same Jesus that promised that He is preparing a place for us, also spoke in the
same passage, these words. *"Verily, verily, I say unto you,
He that believeth on me, the works that I do shall he do
also; and greater works than these shall he do; because
I go to my Father. And whatsoever you shall ask in my
name, that will I do, that the Father may be glorified in
the Son. If you shall ask anything in my name, I will do
it."* I don't hear many pastors talking about this portion of
John 14.

Are we preaching Jesus came to **set at liberty them that
are bruised?** Well, if you're not preaching deliverance
to the captives then you are not preaching this, because
they are linked. What powerful gospel words are in this
declaration by Jesus. SET AT LIBERTY. Is this not the es-
sence of the gospel? Liberation by the Lord Jesus! Liberation, freedom . . . for whom? It is for them that are

74

bruised! Preaching deliverance to the captives allowed me to learn that the captives are in bondage most often because of bruises! Bruises, wounds from childhood, unkind words and deeds they were victims of, deep hurts that keep them bound!

Jesus can set at liberty them that are bruised, because He was bruised for our iniquities! A bruise is bleeding beneath the surface! The damage shows up on the outside, but the bleeding is inside, the hurt, the pain, is beneath the surface. Oh, the need for the Church to minister in this area! Bruised for our iniquities . . . our sins? No, our iniquities! Iniquity is evil, wicked, it is often a spirit or the result of someone else's sin. (The mystery of iniquity does now already work), He was wounded for our transgressions (sin) He was bruised for our iniquities. I believe iniquity is a wicked, evil spirit that gains access to a person through the sins of another. Generational sins allows access of iniquity spirits to the children of the third and fourth generation.

The abusive sinful acts of someone else allows iniquity spirits to the victim. He was bruised for our iniquities. The chastisement of our peace was upon Him and with His stripes we are healed. One verse in Isaiah 53 tells us that Jesus paid for our SINS, INIQUITIES, PEACE AND HEALING! The Blood paid for more than we are claiming!

I can't tell you how many I have seen "Set at Liberty" from the bruises of the past. Evil spirits who gained access through some trauma. Evil spirits who keep the bruises painful, who torment because it is their work. Robbing, stealing, destroying and ultimately to kill . . . the Church must deal with this! We must.

We are preaching the acceptable year of the Lord and many are responding to altar calls to receive Jesus as Savior. I know this is what must happen first. But, He is more than just Savior! He is Savior first, but He is also Lord, deliverer, healer, the One who broke the power of the curse. We cannot be truthful in our declaration of the gospel, if we do less than what Jesus said HE came to do.

Will you take a moment and refresh yourself by reading Luke chapter 4. Jesus was baptized and God proclaimed, as the Spirit as a dove descended upon Jesus, *"This is my beloved Son, hear Him."* The beginning of His earthly ministry began by the Spirit driving Him into the wilderness for a face to face encounter with Satan. No big deal, Jesus defeated Satan with the same Word I have today.

However, after this encounter, after the angels ministered to Him, he came back to His hometown and went to the synagogue where it was His custom to worship. Listening for so many years to the scholars and the Scribes, the Pharisees and the teachers of the law, Jesus stood and chose a passage from Isaiah to read. He proclaimed that He was the fulfillment of that prophecy in Isaiah 61. Something interesting happened. The people in Nazareth rejected Him. They actually tried to kill Jesus, but He slipped through the crowd and made His way to Capernaum about 15 miles away.

The people there graciously received Him and they were "astonished" at His doctrine for His word was with power! In the synagogue there, worshiping with the others, was a man with a spirit of an unclean devil! This spirit spoke to Jesus saying, *"Let us alone; what have we to do with thee, thou Jesus of Nazareth? Art thou come to destroy us?. . ."* *". . . For this purpose the Son of God was manifested, that he might destroy the works of the devil."*

76

(John 3:8). Yes, He has come to destroy Satan's work! May I put in Texas terms, what Jesus said to that spirit, *"Shut up and come out of him."* And the devil did!

Now the people in the synagogue in Capernaum were amazed and said, *"What a word is this! For with authority and power he commandeth the unclean spirits and they come out."*

He went to Simon's house and rebuked the fever in Peter's mother-in-law! Word must have gotten out about Jesus. I tell you, pastors, word will get out about the healing and delivering Jesus. Everyone in the city that had any that were sick brought them to Jesus and He laid hands on every one of them and healed them. And devils also came out of many. . .they didn't want Jesus to leave town. They wanted Him to stay. He healed them all and cast out demons!

What was the difference between Nazareth and Capernaum? Why does the Scripture say that "Jesus could not do many mighty works in Nazareth . . . ?" Because of their unbelief! Capernaum – great revival, great change, liberation, deliverance, healing. Nazareth – anger, self-righteous tradition, doubt, disbelief. Nazareth said, *"This is not the message we wanted to hear from you."* They got what they wanted. Churches today are saying, this is not the message we want. They get what they want.

The difference in Nazareth and Capernaum is attitude! Capernaum had a faith attitude, they welcomed Jesus with no strings attached, they were impressed with His Word, His power and His authority. They saw great results. Nazareth refused to believe! Stubbornly decided to stay in bondage of the elders and religious tradition. Every pastor has a choice. Do you realize that if you don't expect the gifts of the Spirit, you will not receive them! We are told to "desire" spiritual gifts. Why would a pastor not desire something from God's Holy Spirit? That is a question I cannot answer.

There is a sleeping giant that must be freed. The Body of Christ is sickly and without power. Pulpits are trying more and more gimmicks to bring people in, to build a great AUDIENCE. What about the ARMY? God's people are sick, they need healing. Many are demonically oppressed. They are hurting and many lives and families are broken. A powerless church cannot minister to these needs. From the outside looking in, we are no different than the world. That should not be! We have an untapped source in the Holy Spirit, but great restriction has been placed on His role in the Church.

CONSIDER THE CALL ON MOSES' LIFE

Do you believe the call on your life is less real than the call on the life of Moses? Do you think Moses may have been a little intimidated, when he was instructed to go into the physical and spiritual stronghold of Egypt, look Pharaoh in the eye and say, "Let my people go"? Do you suppose he wondered about the consequences of being a child of God and taking on the empire of Egypt? Did any of that matter?

The only thing that seems important about Moses' call was Who called and Who promised to go with him.

I believe the call on every preacher's life is virtually the same, to look the devil(s) right in the eye and command, "Let my people go!" That's what deliverance is. It is coming against demon powers, that keep God's People in bondage, in the authority of the Name of Jesus and commanding their release. God's people are hurting. The church is full of sick people. The hospitals record as many Christians as non-Christians as patients, maybe more. The Church should be free! Jesus paid for our freedom. Demons have intimidated our preachers and Christian leaders. We must take back what is ours. The Blood of Jesus Christ has not lost any power, nor will it. The Name of Jesus Christ still causes demons to tremble and retreat. The gates of hell still will NEVER prevail against the Church of the Lord Jesus.

I look around in the churches where I minister and where I attend. There is always a long list of prayer request for the sick. However, it seems the best most churches do is a courtesy prayer on a weeknight.

We take too much from the kingdom of darkness! We have authority to BIND evil spirits just like Jesus did and command them out of people. Spirits of sickness and disease will retreat in the Name of Jesus Christ. We have been given authority to LOOSE heaven's blessings, ministering spirits (Hebrews 1:14), Holy Angels, to minister for us. How about "Let's do it!"

I have sat in church many times over the years and felt in my spirit, "Why do we just talk about what Jesus came to do. Let's just do it. Anybody sick? Would you like to have the elders of the church anoint you with oil and lay hands on you for your healing? Come on!" I feel this in my spirit, why don't we get on the offensive? Why don't we fight demon powers in the Name of Jesus with the intention of winning?

I am talking about becoming an ARMY not just an audience.

God help us!

Chapter 8

KEEPING GATES CLOSED

Keys are for locking or unlocking. Jesus gave us keys to the Kingdom of heaven in Matthew 16:19 and in Matthew 18:18.

Paraphrased those verses would read like this. *"Whatever you speak to be bound on earth, I will bind it from heaven and whatever you speak to release on earth, I will release it from heaven."*

We bind, lock, or restrain on earth by faith, and that faith is honored in heaven. For instance when we "bind" demons in the Name of Jesus Christ, we speak it, God honors it. Demons are restrained, bound, locked by the authority He has given to us in Jesus Name.

Also when we "loose" angels to minister for us, we have spoken it by faith and God honors it in heaven. Keys are also spiritual principles. Insight that we have been given to live a liberated life in Christ Jesus.

This section is aimed primarily to those who have been set free from demonic oppression. However, it is also good information for anyone desiring to live in freedom that is ours through the Lord Jesus. Keeping the enemy out of our lives and keeping the Word of God in us is the focus. Evil spirits must have some kind of legal permission to enter a believer's life. Unconfessed sin is a gate for de-

81

mons to enter. Perhaps the best example of "doors" or entryways is the example Jesus used in Revelation 3:20, *"Behold, I stand at the door and knock: if any man hear my voice, and open the door, I will come in to him, and will sup with him, and he with me."* Obviously, Jesus is saying that we must open the door for Him to enter. He patiently, lovingly knocks, but will come in only when He is invited. Demon spirits must also have a door or gate that we open to allow them entrance into our lives. Evil spirits must honor our will and abide by guidelines spelled out in Scripture. They cannot enter our life by force. There must be legal permission and we give them consent, when we live in disobedience, believe their lies, or when permission is granted by curse.

Gates serve two purposes, keeping something in and keeping something out. What a person lets in after deliverance is totally up to the individual. If gates are kept closed, the enemy cannot gain access! Perhaps the most important aspect of the warfare that we are engaged in is awareness of it. I have put these together in a simple format so that it will be easy to remember. I call it the three "R's", like reading, 'riting and 'rithmatic, these are some basic strategies for walking in the liberty that has been given by the Lord Jesus Christ. The first "R" that I recommend in KEEPING GATES CLOSED is:

Recognize
Recognizing the enemies and their plan of attacks is imperative in this fight. You may have expected me to say HIS plan of attack rather than theirs. While it is the kingdom of Satan that we deal with, we encounter his demonic spirits.

Being aware of the strategies and cognizant of how warfare takes place, is necessary to keep the victory. It is good to know how doorways are opened to demonic spirits and what doorways were opened to allow them access prior to deliverance.

Make some notes about your deliverance, if you can. What were the strongholds? Do you recall the entryways that gave them access to enter your flesh and soul?... (not spirit, we are possessed by the Spirit of God). Being aware of how evil spirits gained legal access to your life before, may help you keep that doorway closed!

For instance, if doubt and unbelief granted them consent before, they may well try to stir that in you by giving you thoughts and suggestions from the outside. You must recognize their subtle attempts to get you to believe their lies. That is, when you have granted them permission! Be aware, stay alert, don't be caught off guard.

I am going to list a few doorways, that is, "consent" from God, permission, or "legal rights" for evil spirits to indwell believers. Here are some of the most obvious ones:

UNFORGIVENESS - likely the most common doorway for demon spirits to torment believers. See God's consent for demons to torment believers because of unforgiveness in Matt. 18:23-35.

ANGER - Ephesians 4:26 (gives place to the devils) Matthew 5:21-25.

RELATED SIN - hatred, bitterness, revenge, resentment, jealousy, rebellion, violence, etc.

SEXUAL IMPURITY - Romans 1:18-31.

DISHONORING YOUR OWN BODY - smoking, drinking, drugs, body piercing, tattoos, breast enhancement, etc. - Romans 1:24.

LYING - this one can be so subtle that you may not recognize it as a gate for demons.

BLASPHEMY

OCCULT - Curiosity or involvement, however innocent, horoscopes, astrology, fortune telling, psychics, palm reading, Ouija boards, magic 8 ball, witchcraft, levitation games, reading tea leaves, heavy metal music, Dungeons and Dragons, similar video games, Pokemon cards, Harry Potter children's books. Books about the occult, pagan deities, Greek mythology etc. The list is long and I have seen doorways from each of these. Masonry, Eastern Star, Rainbow girls, Oddfellows lodge, Rebecca Lodge, college fraternities or sororities etc.

TRAUMA - surgery, accidents, sexual, verbal and physical abuse, unusual fear, horror movies or events, TV movies or programs, videos.

PORNOGRAPHY

DOUBT - unbelief

CERTAIN OBJECTS IN HOME OR POSSESSION

MANY OTHER DOORWAYS
Permission is granted by disobedience to the Lord. Con-

sent is given by making wrong choices and believing the demon's lie. When we accept the lie, rather than believing the truth of God's Word we have granted permission to demons. The same is true, when we choose the curse, instead of the promised blessings. Don't accept the subtle lies of the enemy.

Awareness of what allowed demon spirits access to your life before, will help you keep that doorway closed. The demon spirits that were there by generational curse or ancestral permission cannot return by that permission. Similar spirits can attach to your life by other doorways. The goal is to walk in freedom and live liberated. It is not in the "fighting," but most of it is in the "abiding." Abiding in Christ keeps you aware, because the focus is on the One who defeated the enemy. However, the first of the three "R's" is RECOGNIZE the enemy. Know the demons are deceptive and they do not give up territory easily. Be spiritually perceptive, know they will wage strategic warfare and be ready. Keep doorways closed by keeping your spiritual house clean.

I will give these three "R's" in brief summary at the conclusion.

Resist
Jesus said that Satan is a thief, a robber, a murderer who has come to rob, steal, kill and destroy. Since he has been totally defeated by Jesus, Satan's only power over a believer is in lies, threats and deceit. His demons have come to do the same work, they will rob you of joy, peace, health, sanity, and anything else you allow them to take. A thief must be resisted!
The promise is that if YOU resist the devil, he will flee

from you! The promise in James 4:7 is two-fold:

> Submit yourself to God. That is, abide, focus on Him and obey what you know to do.
>
> Resist the devil and he will flee from you.

It is your obedience to the Lord Jesus in submission that enriches your authority to resist. Humility and faith open the door of your soul to the power of God and close it to the enemy. Pride and unbelief open it to the enemy and close it to God.

It is not scripturally correct to ask God to resist Satan for you, because it has already been done. The Word says YOU do it, and because Satan is defeated, his demons will flee from you at the Name of the Lord Jesus Christ. Jesus spoke these words to the church, *"Behold, I give unto YOU power to tread on serpents and scorpions and over all the power of the enemy and nothing by any means shall hurt you."* (Luke 10:19). Power over the enemy has been given to you and **you** must act on it. The kingdom of darkness understands this a whole lot better than we do, and they know they have to flee in Jesus Christ's Name.

Some of the first words to the church from Jesus were, for us to take authority. He said, *"Whatsoever YOU bind on earth, I'll bind in heaven and whatsoever YOU loose on earth I loose in heaven."* YOU take authority and God will honor it. You must resist the enemy at every turn.

He is a coward. Cowards run when they are resisted, that is exactly what the Word says the enemy will do if believers will resist. Peter says to resist steadfast in the faith. (1 Peter 5:9). I think that involves an attitude of knowing whom you are in Christ! The responsibility lies squarely on your shoulders. You resist, and you can walk in freedom. The third of the three "R's" is the best of all.

Remain

As a pastor friend put it, REST in the Lord. (Hebrews 4) Abide in Him and relax in the promises of God. Martin Luther is attributed as the author of this neat little poem:

Feelings come and feelings go
and feelings are deceiving;
My warrant is the Word of God,
Naught else is worth believing.

Jesus insists that we "abide in Him" because He says, "without Me you can do nothing" (John 15:4-5). David Berkowitz, a New York prison inmate, who was known as "the Son of Sam," was deeply involved in Satanic worship. He was involved in some horrible crimes. Today he is a believer and a preacher of the gospel in his New York prison. I once asked him, if he had experienced a personal deliverance? I found his words interesting and encouraging. "Don, I found the more I filled my life with the Word of God the freer I became." That is also how he REMAINS free from the bondage he once knew, by filling his life with the Word.

It is by resting in Christ that wholeness comes and inner-healing takes place from all the damage the enemy has done. I often say that, if you were to be in my car and I was unaware of it, you might think I had lost my mind. Often I speak aloud to the enemy when I RECOGNIZE his attacks. I RESIST immediately with words like, "Don't even try it, I know what this is. I rebuke you and I resist you in the Name of the Lord Jesus Christ . . . and if you come back tomorrow, I'll be standing on the same Word, I am free and I'll REMAIN free in Jesus Christ's Name."

Another picture of REMAINING in freedom is saying what the Scripture says, confessing the Word, coming into agreement with the Word of God and disagreement with the adversary. This is bringing your soul (mind, will, emotions) into agreement with what God's Spirit in you says. (Galatians 2:20)

There is power in confession. Your salvation came through confession, and restoration to fellowship comes through confession. When you fall, don't linger. Immediately claim truths, instantly confess sin and receive God's gracious forgiveness and cleansing. The goal is to REMAIN free!

Here is a brief summary of how to walk in the liberated life afforded by the Lord Jesus through deliverance.

RECOGNIZE:
1. **Awaken** to Satan's intentions and purpose for your life.
2. **Alertness (Be alert)** to his tactics and schemes that worked before. What gave demons access previously is likely the method they will try again. Don't minimize the enemy, because the warfare is real.
3. **Acknowledge** the Holy Spirit as your daily helper and He will give you spiritual discernment.

RESIST:
1. **Arm** yourself, put on the whole armor God. Eph. 6:11.
2. **Act** immediately. Remember, it is YOUR responsibility to resist. Jesus already did His part for us. He has given YOU authority in His Name.
3. **Attend** to detail. Be specific with YOUR commands in

Jesus Christ's Name. Bind them with authority.
4. **Aggress** - be the aggressor, having done all to stand, stand in the power of the Lord. Don't back down, don't back up!

REMAIN:
1. **Abide** in Christ, for this is the key to finding full peace and healing. He IS life and He IS Wholeness. Abide in Him and rest in His Word and promises.
2. **Agree** with Him, agree with the Word, speak faith. Do not allow doubt a place in your life. The power of life and death is in the tongue. Say what the Word says.
3. **Apply** the Word to your life. Seek to do those things that please Him (Praise, Prayer, Practice). Avoid things that do not bring Him honor.
4. **Associate** with Spirit-filled believers. Fellowship with mature believers, who love the Lord and His Word.
5. **Adore** Him with praise and worship. Make a concerted effort to give honor, praise and glory to the Lord Jesus. Demons hate praise. It is a constant reminder to them of their defeat. It was once their privilege to praise God. They have lost their position in heaven. God deserves our praise and there are promises that accompany heartfelt praise and worship, The Holy Spirit of God inhabits our praises. Praise and worship music will make the demons uncomfortable and often will cause them to leave. Fill your life with praise. Play praise music in your home, your vehicle and in your office. Praise is power in spiritual warfare.

The following steps are suggested for daily use to help you as you grow in Christ and continue in your spiritual authority to walk in freedom and exercise power over the enemy.

FREEDOM PRINCIPLES:

Confess sin immediately. Memorize 1 John 1:9; keep this verse alive in your spirit.

"If we confess our sin, He is faithful and just to forgive our sin and to cleanse us from all unrighteousness," and apply it to your life. . .don't allow sin to linger, it must be forgiven and you must be cleansed immediately. Deliverance is only as good as our obedience!

When negative thoughts come, you must rebuke them and replace them with positive thoughts.

Here is a verse for you to apply: *"Finally, brethren, whatsoever things are true, whatsoever things are honest, whatsoever things are just, whatsoever things are pure, whatsoever things are lovely, whatsoever things are of good report; if there be any virtue, and if there be any praise, think on these things."* Philippians 4:8.

Make sure the thoughts that enter your mind fall in this category.

Premeditated sin will invite demons. Keep your plans Holy and pleasing to God

"For this is the love of God, that we keep His commandments; and His commandments are not grievous." 1 John 5:3 There is an awesome promise that goes with keeping

His commandment and doing those things that please Him. *"And whatsoever we ask, we receive of Him, because we keep His commandments and do those things that are pleasing in His sight."* I John 3:22. Focus on pleasing Him.

Anticipate increased freedom as you walk in obedience.

You must learn to dismiss immediately painful memories of your past and live in anticipation of life without bondage. *"Brethren, I do not count myself to have <u>apprehended;</u> but one thing I do, <u>forgetting those things</u> which are behind and reaching forward to those things which are ahead, I press toward the goal for the prize of the upward call of God in Christ Jesus"* (Phil. 3:13,14).

Never forget that Satan and all of his demons are liars. Learn to recognize the lie

"When he speaks a lie, he speaks from his own resources, for he is a liar and the father of it." John 8:44 One of the favorite ploys of demons is to try to convince you that what took place was only emotional and that you are still in the enemies' grip. *"Therefore submit to God Resist the devil and he will flee from you. Draw near to God and He will draw near to you. Cleanse your hands, you sinners; and purify your hearts, you double-minded"* Gal. 4:7,8)

Trust God daily to help you make correct choices and He will!

"Having begun in the Spirit, are you now being made perfect by the flesh?" (Gal. 3:3).

Use the Name of Jesus, the Blood of the Lamb and your confession of faith against all Satan's temptations and condemnation.

All condemnation comes from Satan. Never believe him. You have been cleansed by the Blood and through the Name of Jesus Christ, you are blood protected! *"And they overcame him by the blood of the Lamb and by the word of their testimony, and they did not love their lives to the death"* (Rev. 12:11). *"There is therefore now no condemnation to those who are in Christ Jesus, who do not walk according to the flesh, but according to the Spirit"* (Rom. 8:1).

Allow the Holy Spirit to control your life; all of you all the time.

Make a conscious choice to make Jesus Lord of every day and every situation. *"I beseech you therefore, brethren, by the mercies of God, that you present your bodies a living sacrifice, holy, acceptable to God, which is your reasonable service. And do not be conformed to this world, but be transformed by the renewing of your mind, that you may prove what is that good and acceptable and perfect will of God."* (Rom. 12:1,2); *"And do not be drunk with wine, in which is dissipation; but be filled with the Spirit,"* (Eph. 5:18); *"Therefore He who supplies the Spirit to you and works miracles among you, does He do it by the works of the law, or by the hearing of faith?"* (Gal. 3:5).

God's Holy Word must have a predominant place in your life.

This may mean not doing something that would take you away from it. Take time, or make time, to read and learn, meditate on God's Word every day. If time is limited, carry Scripture verse cards with you for your free times. Get cassette tapes of the Bible and play it in your car or office. *"This Book of the Law shall not depart from your mouth, but you shall meditate in it day and night, that you may observe to do according to all that is written in it. For then you will make your way prosperous, and then you will have good success"* Josh. 1:8); *"Let the word of Christ dwell in you richly in all wisdom, teaching and admonishing one another in psalms and hymns and spiritual songs, singing with grace in your hearts to the Lord"* (Col. 3:16).

Learn about your battle gear, it has the promise of protection and victory from the Word of God.

"Finally, my brethren, be strong in the Lord and in the power of His might. Put on the whole armor of God, that you may be able to stand against the wiles of the devil. For we do not wrestle against flesh and blood, but against principalities, against powers, against the rulers of the darkness of this age, against spiritual hosts of wickedness in the heavenly places. Therefore take up the whole armor of God, that you may be able to withstand in the evil day, and having done all, to stand. Stand therefore, having girded your waist with truth, having put on the breastplate of righteousness, and having shod your feet with the preparation of the gospel of peace; above all, taking the shield of faith with which you will be able to quench all the fiery darts of the wicked one. And take the helmet of salvation, and the sword of the Spirit, which is the Word of God; praying always With all prayer and supplication In the Spirit, being watchful to this end with all perseverance and supplication for all the saints" (Eph. 6:10-18). Make this so that it soon becomes effortless and is part of your lifestyle.

You must severe ties with old unhealthy friendships . . . this is a must!

"Do you not know that friendship with the world is enmity

with God? Whoever therefore wants to be a friend of the world makes himself an enemy of God" James 4:4.

You can count on the enemy to try to use "whatever worked before" to get access to your life again. You must avoid old patterns as well and break former habits that led to sin.

Be serious in your efforts to glorify the Lord Jesus.

"If then you were raised with Christ, seek those things which are above, where Christ is, sitting at the right hand of God. Set your mind on things above, not on things on the earth. For you died, and your life is hidden with Christ in God" (Col. 3:1-3).

This battle is one of dependancy, be careful to not get confident in the flesh.

Admitting you can't do it all by yourself is not weakness, it is strength. Do things with His help. The lie of Satan is to tell you that you can do it without God. *"I am the vine, you are the branches. He who abides in Me, and I in him, bears much fruit; for without Me you can do nothing"* John 15:5. *"Let your conduct be without covetousness; be content with such things as you have. For He Himself has said, I will never leave you nor forsake you"* Heb. 13:5.

Remember the wiles and the sneaky traps of the devil.
Act in your God-given authority, it will always be honored by the Father, who gave it to Jesus to give to you. *"Therefore submit to God. Resist the devil and he will flee from you. Draw near to God and He will draw near to you. Cleanse your hands, you sinners; and purify your hearts, you double-minded"* James. 4:7,8

Praise invites God's presence and causes the enemy to run.

Praise Him because He deserves it, give thanks to God for His continuous goodness. Psalm 103:6, *"The Lord executes righteousness and justice for all who are oppressed."*

Be ready to receive what is given liberally by the Spirit of God from the glory of Jesus Christ at the right hand of His Father, who is also your Father. Remind the demons that you are an heir of God and a joint-heir with Jesus Christ. You are! *"But the fruit of the Spirit is love, joy, peace, long suffering, kindness, goodness, faithful-ness, gentleness, self-control. Against such there is no law"* (Gal. 5:22,23). *"So Jesus said to them again, 'Peace to you! As the Father has sent Me, I also send you'"* John 20:21).

There are certain things that require diligent warfare.

Criticism, negativity, grieving over the past, over- sensitivity, doubt, selfishness, putting feelings before faith, and lack of genuine prayer are all on the list. Be an outgoing person and help others. Helping others will bring blessings. You cannot allow self-pity a place in your life. *"Now the works of the flesh are evident, which are: adultery, fornication, uncleanness, lewdness, idolatry, sorcery, hatred, contentions, jealousies, outbursts of wrath, selfish ambitions, dissensions, heresies, envy, murders, drunkenness, revelries, and the like; of which I tell you beforehand, just as I also told you in time past, that those who practice such things will not inherit the kingdom of God Let us not become conceited, provoking one another, envying one another"* (Gal. 5:19-21,26).

THE WARFARE IS REAL

As the Body of Christ **we are** engaged in spiritual warfare with the powers of darkness. *"For our struggle is not against flesh and blood, but against the rulers, against the authorities, against the powers of this dark world and against spiritual forces of evil in the heavenly realms."* (Ephesians 6:12 NIV). A great portion of Jesus' own earthly ministry was devoted to casting out demon powers, and this authority was passed on to believers in Jesus Christ. (Mark 16:17). Walking in the Spirit after a deliverance is essential in order to keep a person free. The fact is that Satan is determined to rob us of our freedom and every other good thing we have from God. We must learn to stand our ground by means of the weapons that are at our disposal. (Ephesians 6:13-18).

HE ALWAYS FINISHES THE WORK

It may be that the demon powers from which you are now free have been associated with you for a very long time. The demons have been such a part of your personality and thinking habits, that the flesh must be put under subjection daily before realizing the fulness of your freedom. The Lord will gradually heal your mind and emotions in some cases. The Holy Spirit is always gentle and does not give us more than we can handle at one point in time. But, no matter how long it takes, He always finishes the work that He has begun in us.

Regardless of what happens, remember that Jesus Christ won victory for you nearly two thousand years ago. Satan can only try to get you to doubt this truth or convince you to give up your freedom voluntarily. Do not be defeated by negative thoughts, emotions, or circumstances. *"No, in all these things we are more than conquerors through Him Who loved us."* Romans 8:37.

In order to avoid the enemy's snares it helps to recognize some of his strategy. Four typical methods of attack encountered by people after deliverance can be outlined as follows.

FOUR TYPICAL METHODS OF ATTACK

1. The Scriptures say that **Satan is the father of lies**. Even though they are now outside of you, demon powers may still talk to you. Do not accept thoughts, ideas or guidance as coming from the Lord, unless it lines up with Scripture, unless it gives you peace and is a part of normal Christian behavior. The Holy Spirit never contradicts the Bible, never creates chaos within and never tells us to do strange things. Typical lies from the enemy might sound like this. "You haven't been delivered." "It wasn't real." "It wasn't completed." "You can't keep your freedom." "The demons are still inside you." Or, "God demands that you do such a thing, or else!" Do not believe it. Make your stand on the Word of God. "So if the Son sets you free, you will be free indeed." John 8:36.

2. One meaning for the name **"Satan" is "accuser."** You may find yourself feeling guilty for having had demon powers from your past sins. Remember that all your sins and failings are under the cleansing of the Blood of Jesus Christ, and God has put them out of His memory. On the other hand, you may be told that you are too weak to resist the devil, you are failing God, and you are just a lousy person generally. The trick behind these lies, and the ones discussed above, is getting you to focus on yourself, instead of on Jesus Christ.

No matter what we are or have been, Jesus Christ is perfect and He loves us. Remember that your strength comes not from your own faithfulness, but rather from your faithful Lord. "But I trust in Your unfailing love, my heart rejoices in Your salvation." Psalms 13:5. Relax in God's full salvation for you. The name "Jesus" means "God-saves;" not, "man-must-save-himself."

3. The enemy **may try to intimidate you** with demonstrations of his power. Do not be frightened if things seem to go wrong for you for a while, or if some symptoms from before deliverance seem to reappear. Remember, that if Satan was as powerful as he claims to be, he would have swept us all away a long time ago. The reason that we are still here is that his power, in fact, is very limited. There is only one all-powerful Person and He is the same God, the Father of our Lord Jesus Christ, Who sends us the Holy Spirit to dwell within us, and in Whom we are baptized. We are on the winning side.

4. You may find yourself **tempted with old habits** or behaviors that do not fit in with the Christian life. The devil has a way of making the old times seem rosy to us, just like he tricked the Israelites in the desert into missing the "leeks and onions" that they had left behind in Egypt. Of course, Satan forgot to mention the misery and slavery that went along with those tasty onions. Do not become nostalgic about the past, but keep your eyes on the future as you prepare to enter God's promised land. Jesus Christ did not come to take good things away from you, but rather to bring you real life. *"I have come that they might have life, and have it to the full."* John 10:10b. Put your trust in Jesus Christ and you will have the desire of your heart. Psalm 37:4.

Recognizing the enemy's strategy is helpful, but it does not win the battle for us. It is more important that you learn and practice some positive principles that will enable you to gain ground quickly and hold it. The following five points are easy to remember and will help you tremendously.

POSITIVE PRINCIPLES T0 ENABLE YOU

1. **Focus your attention on Jesus Christ.** His Blood is the most powerful protection in the universe. Moreover, Jesus Christ came and shed His Very Blood, because He loves you. Confess the fact that He loves you, and repeat the following prayer every morning, both in your heart and out loud. "Lord, I cover my mind, my emotions, my body, my soul and spirit with the precious Blood of Jesus Christ."

Talk to Jesus throughout every day, sharing the good things and the bad with Him. You can be sure He will not leave you. "They overcame him (Satan) by the Blood of the Lamb and by the word of their testimony"; Revelation 12:11.

2. **Allow the Holy Spirit** to have his way with you. Pray throughout the day. Let the Holy Spirit show you negative attitudes, habits, feelings and behaviors that need to be changed. The Holy Spirit is God's power given in order for you to become like Jesus Christ. He will show you things through the Bible, through other people, and through your experiences. "And pray in the Spirit on all occasions with all kinds of prayers and requests." Ephesians 6:18. *"But when He, the Spirit of truth, comes, He will guide you into all truth. He will not speak of His Own; He will speak only what He hears, and He will tell you what is*

yet to come." John 16:13.

3. **Immerse yourself in the Scriptures**. The Bible is the written Word of God. The Word of God is a living thing that works in us, even when we may not understand or comprehend fully what we are reading. Read as much as you can, but preferably at least five chapters from the New Testament Gospels each day. If your mental state makes this impossible, then, until the Lord has healed your mind further, concentrate on memorizing a verse from Scripture each day, constantly repeating it to yourself. Select verses that seem to apply to you and you may begin with some verse quoted in this article. *"If you hold to My teachings, you really are my disciples. Then you will know the truth, and the truth will set you free."* John 8:31.

4. **Command the devil** and demon powers, in the name of Jesus Christ, to go away and leave you alone. Make it clear that you intend to follow Jesus Christ no matter what. Above all, do not argue with the enemy and entertain his thoughts, because you cannot beat him that way. Instead, clear your mind by gently praising Jesus Christ. *"Submit yourself, then, to God, resist the devil, and he will flee from you."* James 4:7.

5. **Hang on to other Christians**. The Christian walk is not a solo performance. You will need other people in the Christian Fellowship to support you and edify your faith. This is nothing to be ashamed of, but rather it is God's preferred way. Jesus Christ ministers through His Body. *"Carry each other's burdens, and in this way you will fulfill the law of Christ."* Galatians 6:2. Thank the Father for sending Jesus Christ.

Practice these five FAITH principles, and your post-deliverance problems will be minimal and your progress steady. Remember that God will not abandon you, and do not be discouraged by any failures. Thank the Father for sending Jesus Christ and anointing Him with the Holy Spirit to bring us out of the kingdom of darkness into the kingdom of light.

"The Spirit of the Lord is upon Me, because he has anointed me to preach the good news to the poor. He has sent me to proclaim freedom for the prisoners and recovery of sight for the blind, to release the oppressed, to proclaim the year of the Lord's favor. Then He rolled up the scroll, gave it back to the attendant and sat down. The eyes of everyone in the synagogue were fastened on Him, and He began by saying to them, 'Today this Scripture is fulfilled in your hearing." Luke 4:18-21.

James 3:14-17 gives some warnings about possible gateways:
"But if you have bitter envying and strife in your hearts, glory not and lie not against the truth. This wisdom descendeth not from above, but is earthly, sensual, devilish. For where envying and strife is, there is confusion and every evil work. But the wisdom that is from above is first pure, then peaceable, gentle and easy to be entreated, full of mercy and good fruits, without partiality, and without hypocrisy."

God Bless you as you grow and as you lead others into freedom.

Chapter 9

PERMISSION BY PLEDGES AND OATHS

I almost did not include this information in this book. However, because I came under such attack each time I approached it, and because it literally disappeared from my computer a couple of times, I decided that was a good indication to share what access is given to demon powers by permission of pledges and oaths.

I would guess that 40-50% of the people who come to me for deliverance have demons in their life by permission of freemasonry, secret lodges, college fraternities and sororities. That may astound you but it is true. I really don't believe that the people get involved in these secret organizations for the purpose of inviting demons into their lives. I have seen many, many, healed of various sickness and disease when the curse was broken in their lives.

I have discovered college fraternities and sororities, to be huge doorways for demonic spirits.

One man who is entangled in freemasonry told me, "I just joined so I could help crippled children . . ." Another said, somewhat defensively, "Masons just make good people better." Then there was one Thirty-Second Degree mason who brought his wife to me for deliverance, (I didn't know he was a Mason), he said, "I didn't take any vows like what you have mentioned." His wife blurted out, "If they're so good and it is helpful, why do you keep it a secret?"

You see, it's a trap, no believer can take oaths such as you will read below and remain in close fellowship with the Lord Jesus, it is impossible. Now the noose tightens when the believer is asked if he took such blasphemous oaths and he must either admit that he did, which calls for repentance, or lie. I think you know what most choose to do, and the bondage increases.

I don't condemn people who are Masons, I have many friends who made the choice to join. I do believe they made a choice out of ignorance. Most of them tell me, "Aw, I never go, I just joined because someone asked me to and I thought it was an honor to be considered." Others say, "I thought it might help me in my business ventures and associations, etc."

I would like to see every believer free. I don't think folks who get involved in these occult organizations realize what they are doing nor do they understand what curses they may have brought on their family and future generations. Selwyn Stevens of Jubilee Ministries in New Zealand has gathered some valuable information to help free people from the curse of Freemasonry. I share this with you and encourage you to prayerfully read through it. Let the Holy Spirit give you direction. For detailed information about freemasonry visit the website of Jubilee Ministries. http://www.jubilee-resources.com
Information may be downloaded. You may write to them at:
Jubilee Ministries
Box 36-044
Wellington 6330 New Zealand

If you were once a member of a Masonic organization or are a descendant of someone who was, I recommend that you pray a prayer similar to the one below. Be sincere in your revocation and denunciation of the vows, pledges and oaths. Please read it through first, so you know what is involved. It would even be helpful to have a Christian witness present.

I have seen many people healed of both physical and spiritual maladies as diverse as long-term headaches, asthma, heart problems and many other ailments as a result of a conscious choice to denounce the Masonry involvement

PRAYER:
"Father God, Creator of heaven and earth, I come to You in the name of Jesus Christ your Son. I come as a sinner seeking forgiveness and cleansing from all sins committed against You, and others made in your image. I honor my earthly father and mother and all of my ancestors of flesh and blood, and of the spirit by adoption and godparents, but I utterly turn away from and renounce all their sins. I forgive all my ancestors for the effects of their sins on me and my children. I confess and renounce all of my own sins. I renounce and rebuke Satan and every spiritual power of his affecting me and my family. I renounce and forsake all involvement in Freemasonry or any other lodge or craft by my ancestors and myself. In the name of Jesus Christ, I renounce and cut off Witchcraft. the principal spirit behind Freemasonry, and I renounce and cut off Baphomet the Spirit of Antichrist and the spirits of Death, and Deception. I renounce the insecurity, the love of position and power, the love of money, avarice or greed, and the pride which would have led my ancestors into Masonry. I renounce all the fears which held them in Ma-

sonry, especially the fears of death, fears of men, and fears of trusting in the name of Jesus Christ.

I renounce every position held in the lodge by any of my ancestors or myself, including "Master," "Worshipful Master" or any other. I renounce the calling of any man "master." for Jesus Christ is my only Master and Lord, and He forbids anyone else having that title. I renounce the entrapping of others into Masonry, and observing the helplessness of others during the rituals. I renounce the effects of Masonry passed on to me through any female ancestor who felt distrusted and rejected by her husband as he entered and attended any lodge and refused to tell her of his secret activities. I also renounce all obligations, oaths and curses enacted by every female member of my family through any direct membership of all Women's Orders of Freemasonry, the Order of the Eastern Star, or any other Masonic or occult organization. I do this, Father, in the Name of Your Son, Jesus Christ. Amen"

Information about various degrees and oaths taken.

Hippocratic Oath

I SWEAR by Apollo the physician, and Aesculapius, and Health, and All-heal, and all the gods and goddesses, that, according to my ability and judgment, I will keep this Oath and this stipulation to reckon him who taught me this Art equally dear to me as my parents, to share my substance with him, and relieve his necessities if required; to look upon his offspring in the same footing as my own brothers, and to teach them this art, if they shall wish to learn it, without fee or stipulation; and that by precept, lecture, and every other mode of instruction, I will impart a knowledge of the Art to my own sons, and those of my teachers, and to disciples bound by a stipulation and oath according to the law of medicine, but to none others. I will follow that system of regimen which, according to my ability and judgment, I consider for the benefit of my patients, and abstain from whatever is deleterious and mischievous. I will give no deadly medicine to any one if asked, nor suggest any such counsel; and in like manner I will not give to a woman a pessary to produce abortion. With purity and with holiness I will pass my life and practice my Art. I will not cut persons laboring under the stone, but will leave this to be done by men who are practitioners of this work. Into whatever houses I enter, I will go into them for the benefit of the sick, and will abstain from every voluntary act of mischief and corruption; and, further from the seduction of females or males, of freemen and slaves. Whatever, in connection with my professional practice or not, in connection with it, I see or hear, in the life of men, which ought not to be spoken of abroad, I will not divulge, as reckoning that all such should be kept secret. While I continue to keep this Oath unviolated, may it be granted to me to enjoy life and the practice of the art, respected by all men, in all times! But should I trespass and violate this Oath, may the reverse be my lot!

I find many doctors do not take this oath, many Christian doctors make similar vows to God, but not to Apollo or any so-called gods or goddesses. I would hope every Christian doctor who has taken this oath would denounce it and make a vow to the Lord Jesus to be His vessel of healing.

The number of fraternities and sororities in college life forbid me from mentioning all of their pledges and oaths. But you can be sure that virtually all of them can be openings for demon spirits and should be renounced and confessed as sin. With the confession, the believer must command the spirit(s) that came by that permission must leave and never return in Jesus Christ' Name.

Chapter 10

APPENDIX

Biblical Curses

EXAMPLES OF BIBLICAL CURSE:

1. Idolatry. (Either making or worshiping an idol.) Deut. 27: 15; Exod. 20:5
2. Incest with one's sister, mother-in law or father's wife. Deut. 27:29,22,23 3.
3. Adultery. Deut. 22:22-27; Job. 24:15-18; Num. 5:27; . Lev.20:10
4. Cruelty to a handicapped person. Deut. 27: 17
5. Oppressing the defenseless. Deut. 27: 19
6. Fornication. Deut. 22:21-29
7. Dishonoring one's parents. Deut. 27: 16
8. Sexual relationship with any animal. Deut. 27:21
9. Defrauding one's neighbor. Deut. 27: 17
10. Homosexual relationships. Lev. 20: 13; Gen. 19:13, 24, 25

Failure, or refusal, to obey God's commandments brings a curse. If we expect to stay free of sin curses, we must walk in obedience to God. Very simply put, disobedience is a door opener and one of the best biblical examples is the Children of Israel. They came totally and completely out of bondage and went right back into another by disobeying God. How can one know if he is under a sin curse?

First of all, has one despised God, or refused to hearken to His voice? God's blessings come to those who are doers of His Word. Curses come upon all who *"will not hearken unto the voice of the Lord thy God, to observe to do all his commandments and his statutes."* Deut. 28: 15. The Bible specifically names many sins which result in curses.

37 Biblical Curses:

1. Idolatry. (Either making or worshiping an idol.) Deuteronomy 27: 15; Exodus 20:5
2. Dishonoring one's parents. Deuteronomy 27: 16
3. Defrauding one's neighbor. Deuteronomy 27: 17
4. Cruelty to a handicapped person. Deuteronomy 27: 17
5. Oppressing the defenseless. Deuteronomy 27: 19
6. Fornication. Deuteronomy 22:21-29
7. Incest with one's sister, mother-in law or father's wife. Deuteronomy 27:29,22,23
8. Sexual relationship with any animal. Deuteronomy 27:21
9. Adultery. Deuteronomy 22:22-27; Job 24:15-18; Numbers 5:27; . Leviticus 20:10
10. Homosexual relationships. Leviticus 20: 13; Genesis 19:13,24,25
11. Sexual intercourse during menstruation. Leviticus 20: 13
12. Marrying a woman & her mother. Lev. 20: 14
13. Rape. Deuteronomy 22:25
14. Children conceived out of wedlock. Deuteronomy 23:2
15. Accursed objects in one's possession.
16. Any occult practice (divination, sorcery, omens, witchcraft, consulting a medium, consulting the dead). Deuteronomy 18:9-13. Leviticus 20:6,27

17. Murder. Deuteronomy 27:24 commandments Deuteronomy 11:28 18.
18. Murder for hire. (Including those who are paid to perform abortions) Deuteronomy 27:25
19. Forsaking the Lord. Deuteronomy 28:20
20. Not serving the Lord joyfully and gladly in the time of prosperity. Deuteronomy 28:46
21. Not reverencing the name of the Lord God, enumerated in Deuteronomy 28: 1-14, 58
22. Presumption in thought that one can disregard God's Word & devise his own way. Deuteronomy 29:19
23. Cursing or mistreating Abraham's seed. Genesis 12:3; Numbers 24:9
24. Refusing to help in the Lord's warfare. Judges 5:23; Jeremiah 48: 10b
25. Failure to give God the glory. Malachi 2:2 1
26. Robbing God of tithes and offerings. Malachi 3 :9; Haggai 1:6-9
27. Neglecting the work of the Lord. Jeremiah 48:10a
28. Enticing others away from the Lord into a false religion. Deuteronomy 13: 18-21
29. Taking away or adding to the Word of God. Revelation 22:18-19
30. Teaching rebellion against the Lord. Jeremiah 28:16, 17
31. Refusing to warn those who sin. Ezekiel 3:18-21
32. Defiling the Sabbath Exodus 31:14; Numbers 15:32-36
33. Perversion of the gospel of Christ Galatians 1:8,9
34. Cursing one's rulers. I Kings 2:8-9; Exodus 22:28
35. Refusal to forgive others after asking God to forgive you. Matt. 18:34,35
36. Child sacrifice (Example: abortion). Deut. 18:10; Lev. 18:21

37. Disobedience against any of the Lord's command-
    ments. Deut. 11 :28; 27:26

Some people dismiss these truths because they are, for
the most part from the OldTestament. Some pastors teach
that they do not apply today. These are Biblical principles
or laws set into effect by Jehovah God. Jesus did not come
to "destroy the law," but to fulfill it. He actually broad-
ened it and made it spiritual, as well as physical.

Remember what he said about adultery, murder and anger.
The law says. . .but I say." While the law condemns adultery Jesus included "looking upon a woman with lust in
one's heart." The law says do no murder, Jesus said, "Don't
be angry" showing that anger is the seed of murder. He did
not "destroy the law". . .He fulfilled it and widened its
scope.

The simplest way to determine whether or not one is under a curse is by comparing his life to the blessings God
has promised to those who love Him. If one is not blessed,
he is cursed. How does your life measure up to the blessings enumerated in Deuteronomy 28: 1-14? Are you "set
on high" by God, a lender and not a borrower, the head and
not the tail? Is your life characterized by fruitfulness? Do
you prosper – coming and going? Are you free from the
harassment of enemies – both natural and spiritual? Is your
life a success? Is your relationship with God gratifying;
are you recognizing and fulfilling His purposes? These are
the earmarks of a blessed life. If one is not enjoying the
blessing, then he is suffering the curse. There is no in-
between.

Yet another way to determine, if curses are in operation,

is to look for the effects of curses. Common effects of curses are poverty, barrenness, pestilence, chronic sickness, failure, defeat, humiliation, insanity, torment, perpetual traumas, spiritual hindrances, domination by others and abandonment by God and others. (See: Deuteronomy 28:20-68).

GROUPING OF VARIOUS EVIL SPIRITS

ABANDONMENT
Isolation
Loneliness
Not Wanted
Not Belonging Victim

ADDICTIONS
Alcohol
Caffeine
Dependencies
Downers/Uppers
Cocaine
Escape
Food
Gambling
Marijuana
Nicotine
Non-prescription
 Drugs
Prescription Drugs
Pornography
Sports
Street Drugs
Television
Tranquilizers
Video Games

ANGER
Frustration
Hatred Rage
Resentment
Temper
Tantrums
Spoiled Little Boy/Girl

ANXIETY
Burden
False Responsibility
Fatigue
Heaviness

Nervousness
Restlessness
Weariness
Worry

BITTERNESS
Blaming
Complaining
Critical Judging
Gossiping
Murmuring
Ridicule
Unforgiveness
Irrational
   condemnation

COMPETITION
Driving
Jealousy
Possessiveness
Striving
Pride

CONFUSION
indecision
lack of focus
ADD
ADHD
OCD
disconnected thoughts
memory lapses
inability to conclude
perception problems
thought interruption
unable to grasp simple
truth

DECEPTION
Confusion
Lying

Self Deception

DEPRESSION
Despondency
Despair
Discouragement
Hopelessness
Insomnia
Over Sleeping
Self Pity
Suicide Attempt
Suicide Fantasies
Withdrawal

ESCAPE
Fantasy
Forgetfulness
Lethargy
Passivity
   Procrastination
   Withdrawal

FEARS
Anxiety
Burdens
Heaviness
Horror Movies
Superstition
 Phobias
   of Authorities
   of Failure
   of Man
   of Punishment
   of Death
   of Rejection
   Over- sensitivity
   of Infirmities
   of Cancer
   of Heart Attack
   of Diabetes

of Being a Victim
Irrational concerns
Worry

FINANCIAL
  PATTERNS
Compulsive shopping
Greed
Inability to plan and
  save
Irresponsible Spending
Job Failures
Job Losses
Poor financial
  decisions
Poverty
Stinginess

GREED
Cheating
Covetousness
Idolatry
Stealing
Misrepresentation
Fraud

GRIEF
Loss
Sadness Sorrow
Suffering

INFIRMITIES/
  DISEASES
Accidents (falls, cars,
  etc.)
Arthritis
Asthma
Barrenness
Cancer
Diabetes
Family History/disease
Fatigue
Fibromialga

Heart disease
Hypertension
Miscarriage
Mental illness
Migraines
Physical Abnonnalities
Premature Death
Skin diseases/rashes

MENTAL ILLNESS
Craziness
Compulsions
Confusion
Hallucinations
Hysteria
Insanity
Obsessive Comp Dis.
Paranoia Schizophrenia
Senility
Institutionalized
Shock treatments
Mental anguish

OCCULT
Astrology
Automatic Writing
Black Magic
Clairvoyance ,
Casting a Spell or Hex
Chanting
Crystal Ball
Dispatching Demons
Divination
Eight Ball
ESP
Fortune Telling
Fraternities
Freemasonry & Similar
Hand writing Analysis
Horoscopes
Hypnosis
Levitation

Mental Telepathy
Made a blood pact
Made a bloody oath or
  vow
Necromancy
Owned heavy-metal
  music
Owned occult jewelry
New Age
Non-Christian
  Exorcism
Ouija Board
Palm Reading
Past Life Readings
Pendulum
Psychic Healing
Read occult/witchcraft
  books
Science Fantasy
Seen any horror
  movies
Seen any science
  fantasy
Sororities
Seances
Sorcery
Spirit Guide(s)
Spiritism
Tarot Cards
Tea Leaves
Transendental
  Meditation
Visited pagan temples
Visited Indian burial
  grounds
Voodoo
Water Witching
White Magic
Witchcraft
Yoga

SEXUAL SINS
Demonic Sex

116

Exposure
Fornication
Frigidity
Homosexuality
Incest
Lesbianism
Lust/Fantasy
Lust Masturbation
Pornography
Premarital Sex
Prostitution/Harlotry
Rape
Seduction
Sexual Abuse

SHAME
Condemnation
Embarrassment
Guilt
Self Accusation
Self disgust/reproach

PRIDE
Arrogance
Self Importance
Vanity
False self worth

REBELLION
Insubordination
Lying
Stubbornness

Undermining

REJECTION
Perceived rejection
Perfectionism
Self Rejection

RELIGION
Antichrist
Cults
Legalism/Rules
Tradition

STRIFE
Arguing
Bickering
Cursing
Dissension
Disagreement
Mocking

SURGERIES
Anesthesized
Childhood C-sections
Difficult birth
Epidurals

TRAUMA
Accident
Emotional Abuse
Loss
Physical Abuse

Sexual Abuse
Verbal Abuse
Violence

UNBELIEF
Doubt
Disbelief
Rationalism
Skepticism
Unbelief

UNWORTHINESS
Inferiority
Self Hate
Self Condemnation
Self Mutilation

VIOLENCE
Feuding
Physical harm
Threats
Murder
Retaliation
Torture

DEMONIC SPIRITS IDENTIFIED IN SCRIPTURE

Old Testament

Jealous spirit -Numbers 5:14

Different spirit - Numbers 14:24

Sorrowful spirit - I Samuel 1:15

Evil spirit-1 Samuel 16:14-23

Lying spirit - 1 Kings 22:22

Spirit of Cyrus (King of Persia) -
2 Chron 36:22, Ezk 1:1

Broken spirit-Proverbs 17:22

Wounded spirit - Proverbs 18:14

Hauty spirit (defiant/ rebellious) -
Ecclesiates 7:8

Spirit of Egypt - Isaiah 19:3

Spirit of deep sleep - Isaiah 29:10

Destroying spirit - Jeremiah 51:1

Spirit of the kings of Medes -
Jeremiah 51:11

One's own spirit/human spirit
- Ezekiel 13:3

Spirit of harlotry - Hosea 4:12/5:3

Spirit of falsehood - Micah 2:11

Unclean spirit - Zechariah 13:2

New Testament

Spirit of unclean demon - Luke
4:33

Foul spirit/deaf and dumb spirit -
Mark 9:25

Spirit of infirmity-Luke 13:11

Spirit of divination,Acts 16:16

Evil spirit - Acts 19:15-16

Spirit of lust - Romans 1:24

Spirit of bondage - Romans 8:15

Spirit of slumber - Romans 8:11

Spirit of man - 1 Corinthians 2:11

Spirit of the world-1 Cor 2:12

Demonic spirit - 1 Cor 10:20-21

Spirit of the devil - Eph 6:11-12

Spirit in children of disobedience -
Eph. 2:2

Spirit of fear - 1 Timothy 1:7

Seducing or deceiving spirit -
I Timothy 4:1

Spirit of antichrist-1 John 4:3

Spirit of error - 1 John 4:6

Note these simple but often neglected truths from God's Word.

The 12 Disciples were given authority to heal the sick, cleanse the lepers, to cast out demons and to raise the dead! **Matthew 10:1-8**

The "70" disciples, (representative of all Christians) are sent out with authority. They marveled that even the spirits are subject unto them. **Luke 10:1, 8, 9 17-19**

Believers are given anointing for discerning the spirits. **I John 2:20,27**

We are shown how spirits not of God can be identified. **I John 4:1-3**

Our weapons are spiritual and mighty through God. We can tear down strongholds built in the mind by the enemy. **2 Corinthians 10:3-5**

It is FAITH's shield that resists the demons fiery darts. **Ephesians 6:16**

The Holy Spirit has been sent to lead us and to guide us into all truth. **John 16:13**

Holy presence and power is revealed when the enemy is shattered. **Psalms 18:37-42**

Jesus commissioned believers to `cast out devils in His Name'. **Mark 16:17**

We are warned not to rejoice in the power that has been given to us but rather to rejoice in our identity in Christ. **Luke 10:20-24**

Evil spirits are most often responsible for sickness and disease. **Luke 8:2, Luke 13:11**

Demon oppression is demons in the soul (mind, will and emotions), or the flesh or attached to a life.
Psalms 116, Acts 10:38
The One who abides in us is greater than the "strongman" **(1 John 4:4)** and we are commissioned to bind Satan.
Matt 12:29, Luke 11:22
Resist the devil . . . stand firm in your faith. **1 Peter 5:9**

Over the years I have encountered thousands of demon powers and have been able to identify their names, their functions and the access to a person's life. In the course of multitudes of deliverances I have categorized these names. Beside the name I have listed the demons function in the particular individual's life. I am going to list a few beginning with names starting with "A".

If you would like a copy of the complete list you can get them by visiting our website and sending an e-mail to us. The web address is **www.dondickerman.com** .
Our e-mail address is **don@dondickerman.com**

THE FOLLOWING IS IS A PARTIAL LISTING. . .
go to **www.dondickerman.com** to request complete list or write to:

DON DICKERMAN

Box 575

Hurst, TX 76053

COMPILATION OF DEMON NAMES, GENERAL INFORMATION

AARON-Ouija Board

ABA-deceit, anger

ABDULLAH-anti-Christ

ABETHOR-Fear manifested to candidate as skeleton

ABBADON-King

ACCUSATION-
    ASHTAROTH (Semetic
    goddess of fertility)
    Judges 2:13;

ACCUSATION, CRITICISM.
    See also SELF-
    ACCUSATION

ACCUSER OF BRETHREN-
SATAN; Rev .12: 10

ADDICTIVE-COMPULSIVE-
    See related demons of
    ALCOHOL DRUGS
    GLUTTONY, nicotine,
    medication caffeine

ADBOA-Fatigue, Alzheimer
    disease

**ADIRONDAK-Territorial
spirit over North America**

ADULTERY -See SEXUAL
    IMPURITY

AFFECTATION-See related

demons of DRAMATICS ,
PLAY -ACTING,
ATTENTION-GETTING;
theatrics, sophistication,
pretension

AFMAIR-fist of fire/anger

AGITATION-See
IMPATIENCE

AHAB-turmoil

**AHMIGIHAD-Territorial
spirit over Carter County
Ok. Dragon**

ALLAH-anti-Christ, havoc

ALLABHUE-deception, Koran

ALAZARETH-serpent,
    PYTHON

ALCAZAR-kill, alcohol spirit,
    accidents, destruction

ALCOHOL- ALVAIZEITAN:
    ALCOHOL, DRUGS,
    MURDER; under
    WASRIDRIANUMCO,
    controller of DRUGS,
    ROCK MUSIC. See also
    ESCAPE, ADDICTIVE
    COMPULSIVE; Break the
    curse of Noah and throw
    out the spirits of Noah
    (Genesis 9:24); and
    associated spirits of wine
    drinking, strong drink,

122

rage, deception, and
stupidity (Proverbs 20:1).
ALDIN-Blessing thief
ALBATROSS-prince, pain
ALLACAZAR-kill, destroy
ALLERGIES-MERIHAM: a
    controller of; hay fever,
    sore throat, asthma, all
    kinds of allergies,
    controller of females
ALLUM-allergies
ALI-deception
AMDEN-Chaos-Druid-
    Scotland
AMULETS--See OCULT and
WITCHCRAFT
ANATHIAS-Rejection
    (incubator)
ANDREA-Lesbian ANNA-
    Rejection
ANNABETH-confusion
ANEXUS-channel/pull in
    others communicate with
    spirits
ANGER-See BITTERNESS,
    PERFECTION
ANIMALS -INORDINATE
    AFFECTION FOR
    ANIMALS   See also
    INSECURITY,
SCHIZOPHRENIA, SEX with

ANIMALS; DOG-
DALMATIAN, a power
which enters dogs;
DOBERMAN, vicious
spirit DRAGON-
LUCIFER, SATAN,
DEVIL; Rev. 20:2; Isaiah
    14:12 LION--ELIAMOS :
    lion worship,OWLS-
    HULDA: puts demons into
    idols & owls,
IDOLATRY, REPTILES-
    ELDEBO LO, SEA
    SERPENT LEVIATHAN,
    Isa. 27:1, Job 41:3; King
    of the children of Pride;
    See PRIDE SERPENT-
    DEVIL, SATAN; Rev.
    12:9; 20:2 SNAKE &-
    SHITON , SHYTON :
    BACK or SPINAL PAIN:-
    Jeanne Dixon ' s snake
    SNAKES, SCORPIONS--
    APPOLYON , ruling
prince of fear SCORPION
    SPIRITS, writhing like a
    nest of snakes in the
    abdomen; all kinds of
    FEARS and VANITY
    WOLF - EL LOBO,
    werewolf: associated with

HUMAN SACRIFICE,
ANTI-CHRIST,
TUSCHON: fights against
JESUS Christ; always
accompanied by POWER
and STRENGTH
(Ijn.2:18;2:22;4:3; II Jn.7)
ANTI-SUBMISSIVE-
NESS-See REBELLION,
JEZEBEL,
SCHIZOPHRENIA
ANXIETY -See WORRY
ANTONE-Freemasonry curse,
foothills of Ireland; clan-
clashes
ANUTHEM-miscarriage
APOLLYON-Satan's first,
KING of bottomless pit
APPRENSION-See WORRY
ARCHER-Territorial over
marriages-reports to
Cameron
ARGUMENT-See STRIFE,
COMPETITION
ARLO-abandonment
ARROGANCE-See PRIDE
ARTHRITIS-Gal. 3 : 13-14:
we are redeemed from
curse of law which is
Deut. 28: 35; Job 4: 3-4;
Psa.145:14; 146:7-8; Prov.

14:30;16:24;Isa.35:3;
Heb.12:12-13, source is
often ROOT OF
BITTERNESS, ANGER,
UNFORGIVENESS,
HATRED
ARMADEX- estrogen
inhibitor
ARTIMUS-heart palpitation,
indigestion
ATOL-mitral valve disorder
ATTOTIT-confusion
ASHANTA-stress
ASHLEIGH-worship robber
ASMODAUS-suicide, murder,
killing
ASMODES-blindness, eye
trouble
ASTHMA-MERIHAM, a
controller: hay fever,
asthma, sore throat, all
kinds of allergies;
controller of females (Ps.
91:3; lam. 3: 56; Joel 2:32;
Acts 17:25b) See
ALLERGY Scriptures
ASTRAL PROJECTION-
PYROX, a prince: able to
project 16 minds into one;
(also KARPAY),
CAPTAINTIO a

Nephilim; Gen.6:4,
fallen angels, giants in the
earth. GREEN
PHANTOM: reincarnation
of mind into mind
JUVART: TISIPHONE;
tessiphon: mind control,
VERONO: mind control
ALATO; NEGAERA; TYSEL;
Ezek13:20
ASTROLOGY -See OCCULT,
WITCHCRAFT
MAZZAROTH - 12 signs,
Job 38 : 32; Isa.47:13-14
ASWERTURON-Depression
ATTENTION GETTING;
VOLAIRE, VOLTAIRE, a
prince: emotional
problems, game playing:
see SCHIZOPRHRENIA,
AFFECTATION

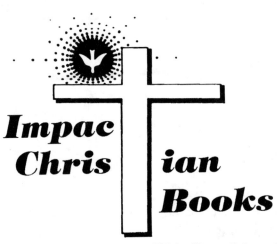

Impact Christian Books

332 Leffingwell Ave., Suite 101
Kirkwood, MO 63122

AVAILABLE AT YOUR LOCAL BOOKSTORE, OR YOU MAY
ORDER DIRECTLY. Toll-Free, order-line only M/C, DISC,
or VISA 1-800-451-2708.

Visit our Website at *www. impactchristianbooks.com*

Write for *FREE* Catalog.